Exclusively KAMADO

 Innovative Recipes for Your Ceramic Smoker and Grill

Paul Sidoriak

Ulysses Press

Published by
Ulysses Press
P.O. Box 3440
Berkeley, CA 94703
www.ulyssespress.com

ISBN: 978-1-61243-450-6
Library of Congress Catalog Number 2015937545

Printed in the United States by Bang Printing
10 9 8 7 6 5 4 3 2 1

Acquisitions editor: Kelly Reed
Managing editor: Claire Chun
Editor: Phyllis Elving
Proofreader: Lauren Harrison
Front cover design and interior design/layout: what!design @ whatweb.com
Photographs: © Paul Sidoriak except on page 58 © Joe Strohmaier
Illustration page 3: © Suman Kasturia
Index: Sayre Van Young

Distributed by Publishers Group West

IMPORTANT NOTE TO READERS: This book is independently authored and published and no sponsorship or endorsement of this book by, and no affiliation with, any trademarked brands of the kamado grill or other trademarked brands or products mentioned or pictured within is claimed or suggested. All trademarks that appear in this book belong to their respective owners and are used here for informational purposes only. The author and publisher encourage readers to patronize the quality brands and products pictured and mentioned in this book. Take special note of the important safety warnings throughout this book, and always use customary precautions for safe food preparation, handling, and storage.

To Chery, thank you for always being there to fuel my creativity.

CONTENTS

INTRODUCTION 1

SNACKS AND APPETIZERS 19

Grilled Crab Cakes 21
Bacon-Wrapped Jalapeños Four Ways 23
Jalapeño Taco Boats 26
Mini Muffin-Tin Corn Dogs 28
Chicago-Style Pigs in a Blanket 29
Grilled Veggie Quesadillas 31

St. Patrick's Day Egg Rolls 35
Duck Confit Egg Rolls 37
Flanken-Cut Beef Short Ribs 38
Zesty No-Fry Buffalo Chicken Croquettes 40
Citrusy Lemongrass Pork Satay 42
Grilled Caprese Salad Bites 44

MAIN EVENTS 47

Moscow Mule Brined Pork Chops 49
Grill Plank Game Hens 51
Beer-Bathed Kielbasa and Kraut 53
Striped Bass on a Salt Block 56
Chinook Salmon Two Ways 58
Reverse-Seared Steak 60
Super-Seared Steak with Whiskey Mushrooms 62
Turkey on the Grill, Montana-Style 64

Turkey Ball Dinner 67
Behemoth Chimichurri Beef Ribs 69
Competition-Style Pork Ribs 73
Hickory-Smoked Beef Tri-Tip 74
Zesty No-Fry Buttermilk Chicken 77
Red Pepper and Bacon-Bathed Chicken
Kebabs 79
Quinoa and Grilled Veggies 81

VEGGIES AND SIDES 83

Grilled Salad with Shrimp Skewers 85
Grilled Corn 87
Hasselback Potatoes 88
Grilled Fingerling Hasselback German
Potato Salad Skewers 90

Prosciutto-Wrapped Asparagus 92
Grilled Artichokes with Crab Cake Stuffing 94
Smoky Salsa 96
Grilled Rice and Red Bell Pepper Patties 98

GETTING CREATIVE WITH THE KAMADO 101

Baked Brie in Puff Pastry with Fruit 102

Insane Grilled Oysters. 104

Grilled Dessert Peaches 106

Game-Day Grilled French Toast 108

Bacon Tornado 111

Chicken Cordon Bleu Sous-Vide. 113

Teriyaki Beef Tenderloin with Green
Onion Skewers 115

Char Siu Pork 117

Bacon Pistachio Pizza 121

Shrimp Scampi Pizza. 123

Gluten-Free Dessert Pizza .125

CONVERSION CHARTS. 128

INDEX. 131

ACKNOWLEDGMENTS 134

ABOUT THE AUTHOR 135

INTRODUCTION

I have always enjoyed cooking, in one capacity or another. I think I started as a taste tester, shortly after I could hold a spoon without throwing it, and then worked my way up to helper. Some of my first chef duties came on special days such as Mother's Day, Father's Day, or other occasions when our brigade agreed that a surprise or impromptu breakfast in bed for the parents was needed posthaste.

Looking back, I doubt if our domestic catering efforts were even edible, and some of my strongest memories are of the messes we made in the process. But we tried and were encouraged to try again. I always did my best to learn from the guests' (my parents') reaction to early-morning smoke alarms, well-done (20-minute) eggs, and toast you could chip a tooth on. As time went on, the smoke detector remained silent, the kitchen stayed cleaner, and I kept expanding the quiver of dishes I could cook to perfection.

A few years ago, when I began cooking on the kamado grill, I felt the same excitement that I'd had when cooking as a kid. Discovering the kamado was like cooking for 30 years and then discovering salt. The kamado adds so much flavor to dishes that it makes me want to cook better every time I fill my grill with charcoal.

There's a funny thread that pops up now and again on Internet forums, about how owning a kamado will ruin you for going out to dinner at a restaurant. You see comments such as these:

"Restaurants are falling short of expectations."

"It was good, but I can cook flank steak 10 times better than what that chef was doing."

And my personal favorite: *"We won't go out very often now, but when we do I'll either order a) Something I know I don't want to make at home, or b) Something I want to make at home and am looking for some inspiration."*

And it's true. Kamado-grilled food often does taste better than what you get in a restaurant! Dining out becomes mere fodder to inspire new dishes at home, and reading the menu becomes an "I can make that" true-false quiz.

Cooking on the kamado grill has been a creative journey for me each step of the way. Starting out, I thought I'd never grill a steak at anything under 700°F—until I learned just how quickly hair singes and knuckles burn. Smoking meat began innocently enough, and then one day I put so much hickory smoke into chicken thighs that the roof of my mouth itched when I bit into one. Even my passion project of pizzas yielded unsightly and inedible results at the beginning, with raw toppings and a crust that looked and tasted like charcoal. I guess you skin your knee along the way and learn from your mistakes on the grill. I've done my best to learn from both my culinary successes and my failures, and I hope that my experience will help you make fewer mistakes and more fantastic dishes.

My personal zeal for creative cooking on the kamado grill has my head on a constant swivel looking for new and innovative ideas. The reward is watching a complete stranger's reaction to my cooking. If someone takes a bite and looks confused, excited, inspired, and exhilarated all in the same breath, I know my food has created an emotion as well as an experience. When someone tells me they'd never have thought of cooking that on the grill, I know I've done something right.

COOKING ON THE KAMADO

The kamado grill is one of the most versatile—and addictive—cooking devices you can own. Part of the mystique is that the cooking possibilities are seemingly endless. With a basic understanding of how the kamado operates, it becomes fun to challenge yourself to see just how creatively you can use it. Baking, braising, broiling, deep-frying, grilling, pan-frying, poaching, roasting, sautéing, searing, stir-frying, and toasting are all methods available for tackling just about any culinary conundrum with your kamado.

Kamado grills are produced by a variety of manufacturers, but they all have certain features in common. The diagram below shows the kamado's typical basic components.

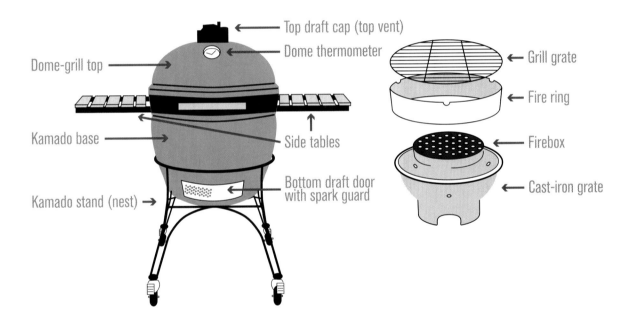

The early kamado wasn't much more than a clay pot used as an refractory-style device to utilize fuel efficiently. Today's ceramic kamado is safer, easier to use, and far more efficient. Stronger handles and hinges are better-engineered to support the weight of the dome. Air circulates with greater efficiency across the coals and cooking surface, and the kamado has a tighter seal during cooking, thanks to high-temperature gaskets.

Similar to wood stoves, kamados all provide methods for controlling the airflow through the grill. Air is taken in toward the bottom of the cooker through the *bottom vent* and exhausted out of the grill through the *top vent (cap-vent)*. Charcoal is ignited in a *firebox* toward the bottom of the cooker.

GETTING STARTED

Hardwood lump charcoal is what's almost exclusively used in kamado grills, partially because it produces less ash than engineered charcoal briquettes. It also produces a very efficient, even heat, adding an unmistakable barbecue flavor. Most manufacturers make their own version, which can be purchased where you bought your grill. National hardware chain stores carry brands like such as Cowboy Charcoal and Royal Oak for a reasonable price, but you often have to deal with massive amounts of dust and very small charcoal chunks in each bag.

At this time, my personal favorite charcoal is FOGO, because the lumps are always extremely large and you have almost no shard pieces or dusty waste. Just recently I tried Komodo Kamado's extruded coconut charcoal made from coconut husks and tapioca starch. Unlike other brands, this charcoal comes in log-style pieces, about 11 inches long and 2 inches in diameter. These logs burn extremely consistently and add very little flavor to food—ideal for a delicate fish or a dessert.

There are various methods of lighting the hardwood lump charcoal that range from primitive and virtually free to expensive gadgets that accomplish the same thing. Regardless of how you ignite your grill, never use commonly found charcoal lighter fluid—it can leave a residue inside your kamado grill that is hard or impossible to remove and will infuse a horrible taste on any food cooked in the tainted grill. My preferred method is immersing an electric starting element into the hardwood lump charcoal and allowing it to radiate heat for about 5 to 10 minutes until it's ignited. If you have a chimney starter where you load the cylinder with charcoal and ignite paper in the bottom, try drizzling a couple tablespoons of cooking oil on the paper to sustain your flames for a bit longer. I tend to stay away from wax-based charcoal ignition sticks that you light and immerse in your charcoal because I don't enjoy the residue that's left behind, which smolders into my food. However you light your charcoal, use caution, do not leave the ignition process unattended, and if you have a penchant to get distracted, set yourself an alarm on your phone to remind you to check the process after about 5 minutes.

STABILIZING THE GRILL

Once the kamado is ignited, it needs to come close to your target cooking temperature and remain there for at least 30 minutes to become stabilized. Stabilizing your kamado is like letting your car warm up on a frigid morning before you begin driving. Although it's not entirely necessary, the kamado—like your car—will operate better when it's preheated to the desired temperature. When the thick walls of the kamado have come close to your target cooking temperature, the heat you lose by opening the dome is recovered much more quickly and your food cooks at the appropriate temperature longer.

For the kamado to become stabilized, keep the lid closed after you ignite the charcoal. You want the kamado to be burning clean, with little or no smoke, before you add food. If you've ever had an old toaster that got smoky because of excessive crumbs, you know how much better toast tastes when the toaster is clean and smoke free. Similarly, stabilizing the kamado lets some of the acrid smoke and any residual morsels from previous cooks burn off from your charcoal, resulting in a cleaner heat source.

GRILL COOKING METHODS

Today's kamado has thick walls that are much denser than those of metal grills. Metal grills have little insulation, so they rely exclusively on the direct heat source to cook your food. Kamado grills, on the other hand, are often quite heavy, and their sheer mass is part of the magic. The extra thermal mass of the thick-walled kamado lets the vessel itself radiate heat onto your food, assisting in the cooking process. Because of this insulating effect, the majority of the cooking on the kamado grill is done with the lid, or dome, in the closed position.

There are four fundamental set-up methods for cooking on your kamado. These differ only slightly, but using the proper setup will help you achieve the results you want.

Direct Cooking

In direct cooking, the grill grate is positioned directly over the coals, with only about a 6-inch space between the hot charcoal and your cooking surface. Other than placing food right in the coals, direct cooking is the hottest, fastest, and most violent way of cooking. Direct cooking is fantastic for searing and achieving a flavorful crust on food. Depending on how hot your grill is running, direct cooking can be very quick—but if you don't pay careful attention, your meal can burn just as quickly.

Raised Direct Cooking

Raised direct cooking is when you elevate your cooking surface inside the kamado dome. Raised direct cooking increases the distance from the hot charcoal to your food, with the additional cooking benefit of radiant heat from the dome of the grill. Raised direct cooking really shines when you're cooking meat on the bone, or thicker cuts of meat where you want the crisping and browning benefits of direct heat but can take advantage of a longer cook time.

Indirect Cooking

Indirect cooking happens when you place a heat deflector/shield (or simply a water-filled drip pan or pizza stone) between the hot charcoal and your food. Indirect cooking is ideal for long, slow-and-low cooking, when you want meat's collagens, proteins, and connective tissues to break down slowly to provide tender, flavorful results. Most recipes that can be baked in a conventional oven—breads, desserts, casseroles, and roasts—can be cooked over indirect heat.

Raised Indirect Cooking

Cooking over raised indirect conditions creates a true baking and browning environment for food. You set up your kamado for indirect cooking with the heat deflector in place, but you raise the grate above the typical cooking height to get your food closer to the dome. Some kamados come with rigs for raising the grate, but there are also many after-market products that will do the same thing. I often just use firebricks to raise

Raised indirect cooking with fire bricks and a pizza stone.

my grate for this style of cooking. Raised indirect cooking is most commonly used for dishes such as pizza, where you need the dough to leaven and bake but you also want the top to be well cooked.

MAINTAINING YOUR KAMADO

One of the benefits of the kamado is that very little maintenance is required to keep it working effectively. Here are some tips for keeping your kamado performing as efficiently on your next cook as it did on your last.

The kamado produces very little ash compared to other charcoal grills, but the ash should be removed from below your firebox every second or third cook. Most kamados come with an ash tool to assist with removal. Spent ash can be sprinkled on the soil around trees and garden plants or just discarded in the trash bin once it's completely cooled.

I take a shop vac to the inside of my kamado about every fifth cook, and before a slow-and-low cook or a high-temperature cook. This decreases the chance that the airflow will be compromised.

Kamado grills have at least one gasket on the lower cooking area; most have gaskets on both the top and bottom domes to help keep the heat sealed in when the lid is closed. You may have to replace your gasket(s) from time to time to keep your kamado operating at peak efficiency. Most manufacturers offer replacement gasket kits with detailed installation instructions.

Most kamado grills have engineered hinges and bands that connect the lower firebox or cooking area with the lid or dome. Double-check the tightness of these bands and hinges before your first cook, after a few cooks, and after any high-heat cook. I regularly tighten the bands and hinges twice a year, when Daylight Saving Time begins and ends.

If you have any questions about how to properly tighten the bands and hinges, chances are that someone where you purchased your kamado will be able to instruct you.

TOOLS AND ACCESSORIES

There's seemingly no end to the accessories you can purchase for your kamado cooker. The accessories that I purchased the day I brought home my kamado aren't the ones I most frequently use today. I'm guilty of spending lots of money on accessories I thought I needed, or that enthusiasts on grilling forums swore by. My recommendation is that you think about what you'll need and do some research before you go crazy buying accessories.

Here are some of my can't-live-without kamado cooking accessories:

Commercial heat deflector being used for raised indirect cooking.

HEAT DEFLECTORS/SHIELDS: Heat deflectors/shields allow airflow to be optimized or restricted so that you can adjust temperature to your preference. They are often made of the same material as your kamado, with a similar thickness to the grill walls. If your kamado doesn't come with this essential tool for indirect grilling, you'll need to purchase one. Or you can use some fire bricks or a pizza stone to the same effect.

TONGS: I have multiple sets of tongs and bring two sets with me almost every time I cook. Why? I tend to set one down and misplace it, so it's nice to have a second set nearby. I use tongs that spring open and can be secured shut for storage. They become an extension of the hand, so you should find tongs that fit your hand comfortably. I have them in lengths that range from 6 to 12 inches. I find scissor-style tongs or tongs with a spatula on one side to be useless, but that's just my opinion.

SPATULA: My spatulas for lifting and flipping food are sturdy, with a decent-size wooden handle about 12 inches long. One of my spatulas has a leading edge that's relatively sharp and a serrated side perpendicular to that. This is nice if I need to really scrape at something or make a cut to check doneness.

Probe thermometer.

THERMOMETERS: Digital thermometers are important pieces of equipment to have for grilling. The probe thermometer that inserts into what I'm cooking comes with a long, heat-resistant cord so I can monitor doneness without opening the dome. A digital instant-read thermometer is also quite a nice asset for quick temperature readings. I purchased a glow-in-the-dark magnetized holder for my instant-read thermometer and keep it on my refrigerator. That way I always know where it is.

GLOVES: Heatproof gloves are always a good idea to have on hand. When you're cooking over high heat, get in the habit of using gloves to keep from burning your fingers. Singed hair is never in style.

GRILLGRATES: GrillGrates are interlocking panels that sit on top of your existing grate, forming a new cooking surface that evens out heat distribution and minimizes flare-ups. A raised rail surface makes gorgeous grill marks. When I use GrillGrates over raised direct heat, they work like a fine micro-adjusted protective barrier that adds a bit of graceful finesse to my cooking.

PIZZA STONE: I've broken many pizza stones over the years simply by using them. Something about the change in temperature encourages cheap pizza stones to crack and break. A number of years ago I purchased a high-quality pizza stone manufactured by the maker of one of my kamado grills, and it has been working fantastically.

SALT BLOCK: Cooking on a salt block is a fun way to transfer heat to food. Made from Himalayan salt mined specifically for culinary applications, salt blocks come in various shapes and sizes. You can find them at specialty kitchen retailers or buy them online.

Be sure to read the care and usage directions before grilling; to minimize breakage, the salt block requires a gentle climb to optimal temperature before you start cooking.

GRILL PLANKS/WOOD PLANKS: Grilling or cooking with wooden planks has been around for centuries—and no wonder, since this method adds wonderful flavor to foods. Native Americans in the Pacific Northwest traditionally cooked salmon over planked alderwood, a method that's still popular today. Now you can buy grill planks in a variety of woods to add different amounts of flavor, based on what you're cooking on the grill.

Grill planks are fantastic with seafoods, cheeses, vegetables, and even fruits, and they make for a stunning presentation when brought directly from the grill to the table. Grill planks can be used two or three times at a low temperature but are affordable, and you shouldn't feel bad if you cook over high heat and only get one use out of them.

DUTCH OVEN: I love using my Dutch oven as an accessory for the kamado; its rugged, cast-iron construction works wonderfully at various temperatures. With a tight-fitting lid, the Dutch oven is a go-to for braising and helps break down flavorful cuts of meat to fork-tender consistency. Filled with water or cooking liquid, a Dutch oven can also make a great heat shield. You can even use it as a drip pan for longer cooks.

FIRE SAFETY

Safety needs to be something you have on the menu every time you fire up the kamado. These grills are capable of achieving extremely high heat. But with a little respect and common sense, your kamado can be operated indefinitely without incident.

Kamado grills come with a screen that slides to cover the bottom vent, allowing air to intake but still providing a protective barrier and preventing sparks from escaping.

This vent cover is extremely important to use every time you cook, especially if the grill is anywhere near grass, wood, or other combustibles.

Keep a fire extinguisher nearby. It's also important is to have a nearby heat-safe surface—such as a sturdy wire rack—where you can remove a hot insert (like a heat deflector) and store it safely. I also do my best to keep heat-resistant gloves and pads, a couple sets of sturdy tongs, and a wrench for removing my grill's grate about an arm's length away, just in case I need to adjust anything quickly.

One of the benefits of using natural hardwood lump charcoal instead of common charcoal briquettes is that when you extinguish the kamado by starving it of air, the remaining charcoal is reusable for your next cook. However, one of the biggest mistakes you can make is allowing ash from previous cooks to clog the internal pattern of airflow. Giving the existing charcoal a good stir will encourage most of the existing ash to fall through the firebox and collect in the bottom of the kamado for easy clean-out. When I reuse charcoal, I always top it off with some fresh charcoal and make sure to fill the firebox to the top for optimal performance, as recommended by the manufacturer. Be careful if you dump charcoal into your kamado directly from the bag—it often kicks up a plume of black dust that's extremely unpleasant if inhaled.

I've found that the majority of sparks occur when you start lighting your hardwood lump charcoal; wear protective eyewear (minimally sunglasses) as a precaution.

Careful consideration should also be taken each and every time you open your kamado grill after it's up to temperature. Over direct heat, anything that has fat content, fatty skin, or excessive marbling will cause the fire to flare a bit as the meat or skin cooks and renders. Of even greater concern are flashbacks. Since most cooking is done with the dome shut, the combustible oils and vapors released by food need to be managed to prevent flashbacks when the kamado is opened. The easiest and most effective way to do this is to open the bottom vent, or draft door, and to completely open or remove the cap-vent from the top of your kamado for 5 to 10 seconds, allowing the vapors to escape. And when you open your grill, "burp" it by first lifting the dome less than 2 inches for up to 5 seconds to let air in before you open the dome all the way. These preventative techniques will significantly reduce the chances of your kamado flaring up and flashing back.

SEASONING RECIPES

Seasoning is simply a matter of preference. Sometimes it simply works best to stick with salt and cracked black pepper. I prefer to use kosher salt in my cooking but feel free to use whatever you have on hand. A word of caution when using seasonings and rubs that have salt added: salt can overpower other flavors, so use sparingly when first trying a new mixture.

The following recipes can and should be customized to your personal taste buds. I'm a big fan of free-styling measurements and ingredients on the fly.

PORK RUB SEASONING

Makes 1¼ cups

½ cup turbinado sugar (or substitute brown sugar)

½ cup smoked paprika

½ cup chili powder

2 teaspoons cracked black pepper

2 teaspoons onion powder

2 teaspoons garlic powder

1 tablespoon harissa powder

1 tablespoon mustard powder

1 teaspoon garlic salt

1 teaspoon celery salt

1 teaspoon celery seeds

1 teaspoon dried thyme

1 Whisk all the ingredients together in a bowl, making sure there are no large clumps. Store in an airtight container for up to 6 months.

RAS EL HANOUT SPICE BLEND

Ras el hanout is a Moroccan spice medley; the Arabic translates to "head of shop," or the best a store offers. A blend of somewhere between 8 and 100 spices, ras el hanout adds a comforting, warm nuance to dishes without being overpowering. Its nutty flavor is fantastic on ground meat, poultry, fish, and vegetables—I've even heard that some people enjoy it on oatmeal.

Makes about ¾ cup

2 tablespoons ground ginger

1 tablespoon salt

1 tablespoon ground cumin

1 tablespoon turmeric powder

1 tablespoon crushed red pepper flakes

1 teaspoon cracked black pepper

1 teaspoon white pepper

1 teaspoon ground cinnamon

1 teaspoon ground coriander

1 teaspoon ground nutmeg

1 teaspoon cardamom powder

1 Place all the ingredients in a bowl and mix thoroughly. Store in an airtight container for up to 3 months.

BLACKENING SEASONING

Generally I don't stick to a specific recipe when making a blackening seasoning. I've even been known to add a spice just because I accidentally knocked it out of the cabinet and it landed near the others, as if it wanted to be on the team. My basic blend generally consists of the following ingredients—adding or subtracting seasonings based on my mood.

Makes ⅔ cup

2 tablespoons smoked paprika

1 tablespoon dried thyme

1 tablespoon ground cumin

1 tablespoon ground coriander

1 tablespoon onion powder

1 tablespoon garlic powder

2 tablespoons salt

2 tablespoons cracked black pepper

1 tablespoon dried oregano

1 teaspoon cayenne pepper (optional)

1 Combine all the ingredients in a bowl and stir well. For ease of use, keep this seasoning mix in a shaker jar with a securely fitting lid. Store airtight for up to 6 months.

STEAK SEASONING

Here's a fantastic steak seasoning that's easy to customize. The base layers can be enhanced by adding fresh dried herbs, such as rosemary or thyme, just before grilling.

Makes 1 cup

¼ cup garlic salt

¼ cup cracked black pepper

¼ cup onion powder

¼ cup garlic powder

1 Mix all the ingredients together in a bowl, combining thoroughly. Store in an airtight container for up to 6 months.

COFFEE SEASONING RUB

This coffee-based rub works especially well on steaks, but it can also be used to add delightful flavor to ribs, chops, and veggies.

Makes 1½ cups

¼ cup finely ground coffee beans

¼ cup salt

¼ cup cracked black pepper

2 tablespoons ground cumin

2 tablespoons ground coriander

2 tablespoons garlic powder

2 tablespoons onion powder

2 tablespoons ancho chili powder

2 tablespoons turbinado sugar
(or substitute brown sugar)

1 Mix everything together in a bowl, combining thoroughly and making sure there is no clumping of ingredients. Store in an airtight container for up to 1 month.

SUV SEASONING RUB

This seasoning is versatile for many things you'll cook on the kamado, and I encourage you to keep some made up in your pantry. I call it the SUV rub because—like a sport utility vehicle—it can go anywhere.

Makes 2½ cups

½ cup salt

½ cup cracked black pepper

½ cup garlic powder

½ cup onion powder

½ cup smoked paprika

1 Combine all the ingredients in a bowl and stir well. For convenience you can store this seasoning rub in a shaker jar that has a securely fitting lid for up to 1 month.

BACON POWDER

Bacon powder is the frozen, pulverized version of bacon strips. When mixed with a lean meat, these tiny granules add layers of flavor while keeping your dish moist. Even small amounts of these frozen pebbles pack lots of flavor.

Makes 1½ cups

4 strips thick bacon, finely diced

1 Line a 9 x 13-inch baking tray with parchment paper. Spread the diced bacon out on the paper so that none of the pieces are touching.

2 Place in the freezer for 2 to 4 hours, until completely hardened.

3 Remove from the freezer and quickly transfer to the bowl of a food processor. Pulse until the bacon is broken into fine particles, resembling a loosely packed snow cone.

4 Return the pieces to the freezer so they remain frozen. Store in a zip-top freezer bag for up to 45 days.

TEMPERATURES FOR COOKING MEAT

	Rare	Medium Rare	Medium	Medium Well	Well	USDA Minimum (as of 1/15/15)
BEEF, VEAL, AND LAMB						
Steaks & Chops	125–130°F	130–135°F	135–140°F	150°F	160°F	145°F with 3 min. rest
Whole Roasts	125–130°F	130–135°F	135–140°F	150°F	160°F	145°F with 3 min. rest
Ground Meat						160°F
Brisket					195–205°F	
PORK						
Chops			145°F		160°F	145°F with 3 min. rest
Roasts (Loins, Tenderloins)			145°F		160°F	145°F with 3 min. rest
Ham (Fresh, Smoked)			145°F			145°F with 3 min. rest
Ham (Cooked)			140°F			145°F
Butts, Shoulders					195–200°F	
Ground						160°F
POULTRY						
White Meat					160°F	165°F
Dark Meat					175–180°F	165°F
Ground					165°F	165°F
FISH						
Dense Flesh Like Salmon			120°F		145°F	145°F

CHAPTER 1
SNACKS AND APPETIZERS

The kamado transforms ingredients that vary from basic to boisterous into bites of culinary bliss. You don't need a special occasion to make any of these snacks and appetizers on your grill, but many of them work well for small-plate parties, game day, or just as a rewarding preamble to a significant main course.

Some of these nibbles call out for seasonal representation. Bite-size Chicago-Style Pigs in a Blanket are a favorite for opening day of baseball season, while I almost always make Duck Confit Egg Rolls on Super Bowl Sunday.

GRILLED CRAB CAKES

This recipe is a perennial favorite with my friends and family. I know for a fact that I have been invited to dinner parties because of my crab cakes, but their simplicity makes it no bother at all to whip up a batch.

Makes 8 crab cakes

2 eggs

¼ cup Worcestershire sauce

¼ cup mayonnaise

¼ cup Sriracha, or to taste

juice of ½ lemon

1 (16-ounce) can jumbo lump crab, or 1 pound fresh crabmeat if you can get your hands on it

½ cup panko breadcrumbs

12 buttery-style crackers, finely crushed, about 1 cup

1 Whisk the eggs, Worcestershire, mayonnaise, Sriracha, and lemon juice together in a bowl until smooth. Gently fold in the crab to coat well without breaking up the larger pieces. Cover and refrigerate for 30 minutes, or up to 4 hours.

2 Set up your kamado for raised direct cooking and stabilize at 350°F.

3 Combine the panko and cracker crumbs in a small bowl and then gently fold in the coated crab mixture. The crumbs will absorb excess moisture and help bind the cakes. The mixture should be quite moist, but without any pooling of wet ingredients.

4 Line a pizza pan with parchment paper. Using a 2-ounce scoop or your hands, form the mixture into 8 individual crab cake patties; flatten, but do not smash. Lay the patties out on the lined pan, leaving space between them.

5 Grill for 20 to 25 minutes on the lined pan, or until the crab cakes are golden brown and crispy on the outside, moist and firm inside. You shouldn't need to flip them, but take care not to let them burn.

TIP I've gotten to the point where I follow a loose interpretation of this basic recipe, depending on what leftovers I have on hand. I've added grilled vegetables, rice, and even quinoa to the crab mixture. I encourage you to experiment.

BACON-WRAPPED JALAPEÑOS FOUR WAYS

Years ago I swore off the jalapeño. I had always enjoyed it, and then one day it stopped agreeing with me. But after almost a two-decade sabbatical, I indulged the request of some friends and took a stab at making bacon-wrapped stuffed jalapeños on the grill.

The concept was easy enough. Core and seed the jalapeño, stuff it with cream cheese, wrap it in bacon, and grill it. I'm not sure what kind of a culinary reaction occurs when these ingredients get bundled and roasted together on the grill, but let's just say I was back on the jalapeño bandwagon at first bite.

It seems that the jalapeño flavor mellows out on the grill the way a snowbird settles into a winter respite on an Arizona golf course. The pepper still packs a punch, but it's milder after grilling, and the cream cheese and bacon bring a yin and yang of flavors that leave your taste buds blissfully confused.

The following variations are fairly straightforward to prepare. Don't be afraid to experiment with other ingredients to go inside the jalapeño along with the cheese—the possibilities are endless. Follow these basic steps, whichever variation you are preparing:

1 Set up your grill for raised direct cooking and stabilize at 400°F.

2 Cut each jalapeño in half lengthwise and scrape out the seeds. Stuff the halves with your chosen the ingredients.

3 Re-assemble the stuffed halves and wrap each jalapeño tightly in a bacon strip to seal.

4 Grill the stuffed jalapeños for about 25 to 30 minutes. Flip as needed until the bacon fat is rendered and the bacon is crispy but not burned.

ATOMIC BUFFALO TURD

Enthusiasts commonly refer to a bacon-wrapped jalapeño as an ABT, or Atomic Buffalo Turd. It generally consists of the chile stuffed with cream cheese and a little cocktail wiener, all wrapped in bacon. Some people sauce it with a raspberry glaze just before service, but mine never last long enough for any post-sear schmear.

12 jalapeño chiles, cut in half lengthwise and seeded

12 little smoky mini cocktail sausages

6 ounces cream cheese cut into 12 pieces

12 strips bacon

1 Stuff each jalapeño with 1 cocktail sausage and 1 piece of cream cheese. Wrap in a strip of bacon to seal shut.

SICILIAN PIZZA-STUFFED JALAPEÑOS

12 jalapeño chiles, cut in half lengthwise and seeded

6 string cheese sticks

¾ cup prepared marinara sauce

12 slices pepperoni

12 strips bacon

1 Cut the cheese sticks in half and stuff each chile with half a cheese stick, 1 tablespoon marinara sauce, and a slice of pepperoni. Wrap in a bacon strip to seal.

SHRIMP-STUFFED JALAPEÑOS

Recently I stuffed an ABT with a shrimp instead of a cocktail wiener and kicked up the cream cheese with some Cheddar and garlic powder. The result was a smoky, spicy, salty bite complemented by the sweetness of the shrimp. It left my mouth baffled but begging for more.

12 jalapeño chiles, cut in half lengthwise and seeded

12 raw cocktail shrimp, peeled and deveined

6 ounces cream cheese cut into 12 pieces

¾ cup grated sharp Cheddar cheese

2 tablespoons garlic powder

12 strips bacon

1 Stuff each chile with a shrimp, 1 piece of cream cheese, 1 tablespoon Cheddar, and ¾ teaspoon garlic powder; seal shut with a bacon strip.

M-80 JALAPEÑOS

Combining a spicy jalapeño pepper with sweet dark chocolate, salty bacon, and intoxicating brandy-soaked cherries may seem strange but the flavors really work well together.

2 ounces brandy

12 pitted maraschino cherries, halved

12 jalapeño chiles, cut in half lengthwise and seeded

12 (½-ounce) dark chocolate bar sections

12 strips bacon

1 Soak cherries in brandy overnight in refrigerator.

2 Stuff each chile with 2 cherry halves and a piece of chocolate; seal shut with a bacon strip.

JALAPEÑO TACO BOATS

This zesty appetizer can be prepared ahead and cooked just before kickoff to enjoy on game day—or any day, for that matter. Using the jalapeño as a serving vessel is a great way to offer a fun snack that's light on carbs. You can use a variety of stuffings and toppings for these boats, based on what you have on hand. Roasting the jalapeños seems to mellow out their spiciness while intensifying the subtler flavors.

Serves 6

½ cup grated Cheddar cheese

½ cup grated Monterey Jack cheese

6 strips bacon

1 pound ground beef

1 (1.25-ounce) package taco seasoning mix

6 jalapeño chiles, halved lengthwise and seeded

1 cup sour cream

½ cup sliced black olives

1 Combine the cheeses in a medium bowl and set aside. Slice the bacon in half so you have 12 short strips.

2 Prepare the ground beef according to the directions on the taco seasoning package. When done, set aside to cool.

3 Set up your grill for raised direct cooking and stabilize at 350°F.

4 Stuff each jalapeño half with a heaping tablespoon of the seasoned ground beef and a tablespoon of the cheese mix. Place a strip of bacon on top.

5 Arrange the jalapeños close together on the grilling surface. Roast for about 12 minutes and then check to make sure that the boats are all cooking at about the same rate. Cook for another 12 to 18 minutes, or until the bacon has rendered and crisped, making it crunchy and delicious.

6 If you don't already have a crowd snatching these jalapeño boats as they come off the grill, arrange them on a serving platter with the sour cream and olives available for garnishing.

TIP You may want to consider wearing latex gloves while working with jalapeños or other spicy chiles. Chances are that some of the oil from the peppers will get onto your fingers, and no matter how well you wash your hands, it can be quite irritating if you touch other parts of your body.

MINI MUFFIN-TIN CORN DOGS

People go crazy for corn dogs. Maybe they bring back memories of going to the county fair as a kid, or that fantastic road trip where a corn dog was your best culinary option for a couple hundred miles. Whatever the reason, they sure seem to put a smile on lots of people's faces. I like to use cocktail-size franks and mini-muffin pans for this recipe so there's plenty to share with everyone. If you happen to be lucky enough to have grandkids or other "helping hands" nearby, this dish is a great opportunity to make some new memories together.

Serves 12

1 (8-ounce) package corn muffin mix

condiments of choice

SPECIAL EQUIPMENT
mini muffin tin and paper liners

24 mini cocktail franks

1 Set up your grill for indirect cooking at the temperature specified on the muffin package (generally 375°F).

2 Prepare the corn muffin batter according to the directions on the package.

3 Insert a wooden toothpick two-thirds of the way into each cocktail frank, like a corn dog stick. Be sure to leave at least a third of the toothpick exposed, to use as a handle.

4 Insert paper liners into the wells of a mini muffin pan and fill each one about halfway with muffin batter. Set a cocktail frank straight up in each filled muffin cup, toothpick end pointing up.

5 Grill for 12 to 14 minutes, or as suggested on the corn muffin package.

6 Transfer the mini corn dogs to a serving platter. Offer tiny containers of condiments to complete the undersized but big-taste theme.

CHICAGO-STYLE PIGS IN A BLANKET

The Chicago dog traditionally comes with a variety of toppings, including mustard, relish, onions, a dill pickle spear, half-moon tomato slices, a pickled sport pepper, and a liberal sprinkling of celery salt. It all goes into a wider-than-normal poppy-seed hot dog bun. This more petite version doesn't take two hands to eat. It's the perfect snack to serve if your favorite team is playing the Bulls, Bears, Blackhawks, Cubs....

Serves 8

4 dill pickle spears

12 pickled sport peppers

1 (12-ounce) can refrigerated crescent-style rolls

celery salt

24 mini cocktail franks

1 egg

1 tablespoon water

2 tablespoons poppy seeds

1 Set up your grill for indirect cooking and stabilize at 375°F.

2 Setting up an assembly line for this dish is highly advisable. Start by slicing the dill pickle spears into 24 pieces (6 per spear), each a little wider than a matchstick and about an inch longer than your cocktail franks; set aside. Cut the sport peppers in half so they are about the same size as the dill pickle pieces.

3 Pop open the can of crescent rolls and set the dough on a plastic cutting board or similar surface on which it won't easily stick. Use a pizza cutter and a ruler to make it easy to cut the dough into strips. Lay the dough rectangle horizontally on your work surface and cut it into 12 slices from top to bottom. Now make a single cut from left to right across the center of the dough. Magically, you now have 24 dough slices. Sprinkle celery salt over the dough so that it covers well but doesn't clump.

4 Line a pizza pan or baking sheet with parchment paper. Now it's time to bundle your mini hot dogs. With the celery-salt side of a dough slice facing up, place a piece of sport pepper, a sliver of pickle, and a cocktail frank about ½ inch up from the bottom edge. Begin rolling the dough up around the filling. It should wrap around about 1½ times; don't worry if the hot dog ends are visible. Lay the bundle on the prepared pan, seam-side down. Repeat with the remaining ingredients to make a total of 24 wiener bundles.

5 In a small bowl, beat the egg with the water to make an egg wash. Lightly brush all exposed dough areas with the egg wash and sprinkle with poppy seeds. The poppy seeds don't add a lot of flavor, but they'll make your pigs in a blanket look and feel authentic. I'm sure any Chicago alumni will appreciate the extra effort.

6 Place the pan on the grill. You can pretty much follow the directions on the crescent roll package for cooking time. I generally cook these for 10 to 12 minutes, until the rolls are golden brown.

GRILLED VEGGIE QUESADILLAS

This dish offers you a completely blank canvas. Whether you use the ingredients listed below or choose others, there's one common denominator: the combination of roasting and grilling vegetables brings out both sweet and savory elements that you'd be hard pressed to find with other cooking methods.

Serves 4

1 or 2 medium to large sweet onions

1 medium green bell pepper

1 medium red bell pepper

1 medium yellow bell pepper

1 or 2 green or red jalapeño chiles

2 or 3 medium to large firm tomatoes, such as Roma

1 small bunch green onions

¼ cup olive oil

1 tablespoon cracked black pepper

1 tablespoon garlic salt

1 tablespoon garlic powder

1 tablespoon onion powder

1 tablespoon smoked paprika (optional)

4 (12-inch) flour tortillas

½ cup grated Monterey Jack cheese

½ cup grated Cheddar cheese

sour cream, cilantro, and diced tomato, for garnish

1   To prepare the sweet onions, slice off the tops and bottoms, remove the outer skin, and cut into quarters or thirds; the pieces should be at least 1½ inches thick. Cut the bell peppers into quarters from top to bottom; this will leave the stem intact and holding all the seeds, which you can easily discard. Stem and remove the seeds from the jalapeños; if you prefer a little less heat, remove the white inner membranes using a small spoon or paring knife. Core the tomatoes and cut in half. Cut the roots from the green onions but otherwise leave them whole.

2   In a gallon-size zip-top plastic bag, combine the olive oil, black pepper, garlic salt, garlic powder, onion powder, and smoked paprika (if using). Mix well and then add all the vegetables to the bag. Seal and tenderly knead to coat the vegetables with the spices and oil. Set aside.

3   Set up your grill for raised direct cooking and stabilize at about 375°F. Make sure your grill grate is well oiled and squeaky clean. Take a moment to notice where the hotter and cooler spots are in your charcoal. The objective is to achieve a hybridized grilling and roasting scenario. Thicker, firmer vegetables such as the sweet onion can tolerate a little more direct heat than the tomatoes can.

4   Remove the vegetables from the seasoning bag and arrange on the cooking grate. Place the peppers skin-side down to start; the skin seems to provide a protective heat barrier that allows the peppers to roast, releasing a wonderful sweetness as they cook.

Monitor each of the vegetables for doneness, rotating them between warmer and cooler areas. You want to cook the vegetables about 4 to 6 minutes—long enough that the flavors slowly intensify, but you don't want them to become mushy and break apart.

5   When the veggies are done, remove them from the grill and let cool for about 10 minutes. When they are cool enough to handle, finely dice them using a very sharp chef's knife. Mix the cheeses together in a bowl.

6 Lay 2 tortillas on your work surface and spread liberally with vegetables, then top with about ½ cup of the cheese blend. Place another tortilla on top. Repeat the process with the remaining 2 tortillas.

7 Carefully transfer the quesadillas to the grill. Keep an eye on where your grill has hot spots and position the tortillas accordingly. Leave the quesadillas on the grill long enough that the tortillas blister a bit and the cheese melts, about 6 minutes; carefully flip them halfway through.

8 Remove the quesadillas from the grill and use a pizza cutter to divide each one into 6 or 8 pieces. Garnish with sour cream, cilantro, and diced tomato.

ST. PATRICK'S DAY EGG ROLLS

I like to think of St. Patrick's Day as a go-between holiday. It's kind of a going-away party for winter and an early welcome wagon for spring. It breaks up the doldrums of winter and gives even us non-Irish a reason to get together. One way I enjoy celebrating is with this cylindrical spin on the classic corned beef dinner: the corned beef and cabbage egg roll. Corned beef, wilted cabbage, cream cheese, and a sliver of Swiss cheese get rolled up in a wonton wrapper and quickly fried in duck fat on top of my kamado. This hand-held shillelagh of flavor is a fantastic snack to serve on St. Patrick's Day, or any time you're feeling a little bit Irish.

Serves 8

2 cups plus 2 tablespoons duck fat, divided (or substitute vegetable oil)

1 cup finely shredded green cabbage

1 cup finely shredded red cabbage

1 cup grated carrots

salt and cracked black pepper

8 ounces cream cheese

8 ounces Swiss cheese

8 egg roll wrappers

½ pound cooked corned beef, thinly sliced

1   In a skillet over medium heat on the stovetop, melt 2 tablespoons duck fat. Sauté the cabbage and carrots in the fat, seasoning the mixture with a pinch of salt and pepper. The vegetables should wilt and release liquid, which will slowly cook off and reduce in volume by a third or so in about 8 to 10 minutes. Some light caramelization is fine, but monitor the heat so that the mixture doesn't take on too much color. Set aside to cool.

2   Prepare the cream cheese and Swiss cheese by portioning each into 8 equal-size logs, about as big as a AA battery. Chilled cream cheese can be cut to size or rolled and molded into cylinders.

3   Egg roll wrappers often come with directions for how to roll them. I cannot emphasize enough how important it is to add filling ingredients sparingly, taking care

to not overstuff your egg rolls. Lay a wrapper on a dry work surface and finger-paint the edges with water, moistening an area not much wider than your fingertip. Place a Swiss cheese log and a cream cheese log in the center a third of the way up from the bottom. Cover with about an ounce of shredded corned beef and then a heaping tablespoon of the wilted cabbage mixture.

4 Fold the bottom of the wrapper up onto the filling mixture; flop the wrapper sides in toward the middle to make a pocket. Using both hands, carefully roll the pocket away from you so the wrapper rolls up onto itself, forming a seal as it goes. Crimp edges with your fingers to reinforce the seal. Repeat for the remaining wrappers and filling ingredients.

5 Set up your grill for raised direct cooking and stabilize at 375°F.

6 Set a cast-iron skillet or Dutch oven on the preheated grill and add enough duck fat so you have a half inch covering the bottom of your vessel. When you are ready to cook, gingerly drop the egg rolls into the duck fat away from you, to prevent splashing. Cook for about 2 to 3 minutes per side, turning frequently as needed, until golden brown. The egg rolls should be ready in about 4 minutes total.

7 Transfer the cooked egg rolls to a raised cooling rack with a drip pan set underneath. You won't want to wait, but be sure to let the egg rolls cool for about 5 minutes before biting into them. The roof of your mouth will thank you.

TIP Cooking in duck fat or oil over hardwood lump charcoal can be dangerous, so take safety precautions and be smart. Heat-insulated gloves, long tongs, slotted metal spoons, heat-resistant potholders, a fire extinguisher, and common sense are all good to have at hand before you start cooking.

DUCK CONFIT EGG ROLLS

If you are lucky enough to have duck confit on hand and are looking for a unique way to showcase it, this dish is for you. The cabbage, cream cheese, and duck confit are accentuated with the subtle hint of five-spice powder—reminiscent of a stroll through Chinatown. Balance these enhanced flavors with your favorite Pinot Noir and you have a hearty course that's fit for royalty.

Prepare these duck confit egg rolls as explained above for the St. Patrick's Day Egg Rolls, but use the following ingredients:

2 cups plus 2 tablespoons duck fat, divided (or substitute vegetable oil)

1 cup finely shredded green cabbage

1 cup finely shredded red cabbage

1 cup grated carrots

salt and cracked black pepper

pinch of five-spice powder

½ pound duck confit, minced

8 ounces cream cheese, portioned into 8 logs

8 egg roll wrappers

1   Add the five-spice powder with the salt and pepper. Stuff egg roll wrapper similar to the St. Patrick's Day egg rolls using about 1 ounce of duck confit, a piece of cream cheese, and 2 tablespoons of the wilted cabbage mixture. Cook in duck fat until golden brown.

FLANKEN-CUT BEEF SHORT RIBS

Flanken beef ribs remind me of the Flintstones, because they have an almost prehistoric look. Having recently taken an interest in using less common cuts of meat, I thought of the reasonably priced flanken cut as a great change of pace that packs lots of flavor. Bright, vibrant, and well marbled, these are thin ribs cut across the bones, leaving many bone segments. I'm happy I took a chance on this cut—it has a great flavor that definitely got my taste buds out of the Stone Age!

Serves 4

4 flanken beef ribs

2 cups prepared Italian dressing, plus more for brushing

SUV Seasoning Rub (page 16)

1 Rinse the ribs (flanken ribs are cut on a band saw, which typically leaves bone flakes on the protein that you want to take an extra moment and remove). Marinate them overnight in the Italian salad dressing, refrigerated, to help tenderize the meat.

2 Set up your grill for direct cooking and stabilize at 450°F. Take the ribs out of the marinade, letting the excess drip off, and season liberally with the SUV rub.

3 Begin cooking the meat over direct heat. Immediately paint the top with a generous amount of Italian dressing. Flipping the ribs about every 2 minutes and painting them with more Italian dressing, cook for a total of 8 to 10 minutes. You'll be left with wonderfully charred, chewy ribs that have an intense beef flavor. If desired, cut into small pieces to serve as an appetizer or snack.

TIP This is a hot, interactive way of cooking beef ribs. For safety's sake while grilling, it is important to use long, sturdy tongs and to wear heatproof gloves.

ZESTY NO-FRY BUFFALO CHICKEN CROQUETTES

These easy-to-make, bite-size croquettes are ideal to serve on game day, but they also work well as a spicy appetizer for a party. Grilling the croquettes on the kamado is a healthier alternative to frying.

Serves 8 to 10 (makes about 24 croquettes)

4 strips bacon, diced

½ sweet onion, finely diced

2 eggs, beaten

½ cup prepared wing sauce

1 cooked rotisserie chicken, bones and skin removed

½ cup crumbled blue cheese

½ cup sour cream (or as needed), plus more for serving

cooking spray

1 cup panko breadcrumbs

¼ cup melted butter

1 Prepare your grill for raised direct heat and stabilize at 375°F.

2 In a cast-iron skillet placed on the hot grill, render down the bacon. Remove the bacon from the pan and set aside, leaving the drippings in the skillet. Sweat down the finely diced sweet onion slowly in the leftover bacon drippings until translucent. Remove and let cool.

3 In a large mixing bowl, combine the cooled bacon bits and onion with the beaten eggs and the wing sauce.

4 To prepare the chicken meat, pulse it in a food processor until the pieces are smaller than a fine dice and the mixture takes on an almost fibrous look. The same consistency can be achieved with a sharp knife and lots of chopping, but it's a lengthy process. Using both the white and dark meat gives a balance of flavor and texture.

5 Fold the chicken bits and crumbled blue cheese into the egg mixture until well incorporated, adding sour cream as needed for additional moisture. Cover and refrigerate for at least 30 minutes to let the chicken get acquainted with its spicy neighbors.

6 Coat a baking sheet with cooking spray. In a small bowl, mix the panko crumbs with the melted butter until all the crumbs are well coated. Take a heaping tablespoon of the chicken mixture and roll it in your hands to form a ball about 2 inches in diameter. Roll the ball in the crumbs to form a thin, even coating. Being careful to preserve the round shape, place the lightly breaded croquette on the prepared baking sheet. Repeat the process for the rest of the chicken mixture.

7 Set the pan near the top of the kamado dome and cook the croquettes for 20 minutes. Top with dollops of sour cream to serve.

TIP While buying a precooked rotisserie chicken is certainly convenient, cooking your own whole chicken is a great way to stretch your food dollars. I slowly boil the chicken with carrots, onion, celery, and some favorite spices. You can grill or roast a chicken just as easily.

CITRUSY LEMONGRASS PORK SATAY

I picked up a behemoth blender recently and have been trying to use it in other ways than just mixing drinks. For this recipe, the big blender makes short work of mincing the marinade ingredients.

Serves 8 to 10

PORK MARINADE

2 stalks lemongrass, trimmed and coarsely chopped

zest and juice from 1 lime

2 medium shallots, coarsely chopped

5 tablespoons coarsely chopped garlic

1 serrano or other hot chile, seeded and roughly chopped

3 tablespoons Sriracha

3 tablespoons sugar

¼ cup fish sauce

¼ cup low-sodium soy sauce

¼ cup prepared Italian salad dressing

1 teaspoon cracked black pepper

2 pounds pork loin or tenderloin, cut into 2-inch strips

1 To make the marinade, place all the ingredients except the pork in a blender and blend until everything is finely chopped. Set aside.

2 Thread the pork cubes onto skewers, about two per skewer. Place in a baking pan and pour the marinade over them, making sure all the pork gets covered. Refrigerate, covered, for at least 2 hours, or up to a day.

3 Set up your grill for direct cooking and stabilize at 450°F.

4 Arrange the skewers on the grill and cook for 6 to 8 minutes. Turn the skewers as needed to evenly cook the pork. The meat will pick up a rich, caramel, charred color, and the oils from the lemongrass will release a citrusy aroma.

TIP The pork plays nicely with the spicy, citrus flavors of the marinade. This marinade also works wonderfully to flavor portabella mushrooms, which can easily be grilled at the same time.

GRILLED CAPRESE SALAD BITES

Combining two of the best things about the warmer months—grilling and fresh-from-the-garden veggies—seems like a winning plan to me. I love to show off the bounty from my garden, and this Caprese salad presents freshness from the peak of the growing season. This is a quick-and-hot cooking process that takes advantage of the radiant heat from the kamado dome to melt the cheese and caramelize the tomatoes a bit. Roasting coaxes forward additional flavor that you don't normally taste when tomatoes are raw.

Serves 6

3 tablespoons balsamic vinegar

1 crusty baguette

olive oil

garlic salt

SPECIAL EQUIPMENT
2 well-soaked grill planks

chiffonade of fresh basil leaves

2 or 3 firm tomatoes, thinly sliced

4 ounces fresh mozzarella, cut into thin disks

cracked black pepper

1 To prepare the balsamic vinegar reduction, heat the vinegar on the stovetop in a small saucepan over low heat. Heat for about 4 minutes to slowly reduce to about 1 tablespoon; remove from the heat and set aside.

2 Set up your grill for raised direct cooking and stabilize at 450°F.

3 Cut 6 inch-thick rounds from the baguette and lightly brush both cut sides with olive oil. Season each with a pinch of garlic salt and arrange the slices on a grill plank. Place a few ribbons of basil down followed by a tomato slice. Cover with a mozzarella disk. Sprinkle with pepper.

4 Just before grilling, top each round with a pinch each of black pepper and garlic salt and a few drops of olive oil. Set the plank on the kamado and grill for 5 to 7 minutes.

5 Use the grill plank as a nontraditional serving platter. At tableside just prior to service, top the salad bites with a few final ribbons of basil and a drizzle of the balsamic vinegar reduction.

CHAPTER 2

Main-event dishes are the crescendo of creative kamado cooking. All the extra little things you do to make a dish exciting are accentuated by the flavors, colors, and textures added when you use the kamado grill.

Main-event dishes take sometimes-mundane ingredients and put them on the red carpet. A simple pork chop dons a tux when it dives into a Moscow mule brine, becoming so juicy and flavorful that you'll hug your butcher the next time you're at the market.

Chicken on the bone is transformed when it's slowly grilled at a low temperature. A spa-like soak in herb-spiced buttermilk prior to grilling gives the chicken a full-body massage, resulting in amazing texture and a skin that's as crunchy as a potato chip.

Turkey meatballs incorporating all the flavors of a traditional holiday dinner are as much fun as your team returning a kickoff for a touchdown on Thanksgiving Day. Easy to make, they won't leave you wanting a nap when you put down the fork.

MOSCOW MULE BRINED PORK CHOPS

Inspiration for this dish comes from a joke I had about accidentally spilling my beverage and covering it up by calling it a marinade. When I got to thinking about it, the Moscow Mule cocktail has almost all of the ingredients required for making an amazing brine. This recipe makes the juiciest pork chops you have ever tasted. You'll need to plan ahead to make these—they need to marinate in their cocktail marinade for at least 8 hours.

Serves 2

1 (14-ounce) bottle spicy ginger beer (such as Bundaberg or Cock 'n Bull)

2 ounces (¼ cup) vodka

3 cups ice cubes

2 medium limes

1 cup boiling water

¼ cup garlic salt

4 fresh kaffir lime leaves (commonly found with other fresh Asian ingredients in the produce section of your grocery store)

2 (12-ounce) thick-cut pork chops

Pork Rub Seasoning (page 13)

1 In a medium bowl, make a Moscow mule cocktail by combining the ginger beer, vodka, and ice. Cut the limes into wedges and squeeze the juice into the cocktail mixture, then add the juiced wedges as well.

2 Remove the boiling water from the heat and add the garlic salt; stir to dissolve. Bruise the kaffir lime leaves by folding them a few times; place in the hot garlic water. Set aside to steep for 5 minutes and then add the entire mixture to the cocktail, stirring to combine.

3 Place your pork chops in the Moscow mule brine mixture, making sure they are well covered with the liquid. Refrigerate, covered, for 8 to 24 hours, rotating the chops in the brine every few hours.

4 Set up your grill for direct cooking and stabilize at about 375°F.

5 Remove the chops from the brine and pat dry with paper towels. Season generously with the pork rub on both sides. Insert a probe thermometer into one of the chops from the side so that it goes through the meat toward the bone but doesn't touch the bone.

6 Place the chops on the grate and grill, flipping occasionally to promote even cooking. Typically they are done in 20 to 25 minutes—but cook to temperature, not time. When the pork chops reach an internal temperature of 142°F, remove them from the grill and loosely tent with foil. Allow to rest for 10 minutes before serving.

While the meat rests, consider making yourself a delicious beverage to enjoy with dinner. Perhaps a Moscow mule?

GRILL PLANK GAME HENS

Game hens are perfect size for a light grilled dinner. The game hen is a blank canvas for seasoning, and it's fun to take a nontraditional approach. Cooking the birds on a grill plank brings out additional flavor, and the plank serves as a protective barrier that allows the skin to crisp up while keeping the meat juicy. If you don't have ras el hanout—a spice blend commonly used in curries—regular curry powder should work well.

Serves 2

2 (20-ounce) Cornish game hens

vegetable oil for brushing

4 tablespoons garlic salt

4 tablespoons Ras el Hanout Spice Blend (page 14)

SPECIAL EQUIPMENT
2 grill planks

1 Give the grill planks a long soak in water—overnight if possible, but in a pinch a few hours will work fine. Fruitwood complements poultry; I like to use cherry wood for this dish.

2 Using kitchen shears, remove the backbone from each game hen by cutting along one side of the backbone. Repeat with the other side and discard. This will allow the birds to lie flat on the grill planks.

3 Pat the birds dry with paper towels and then liberally brush with vegetable oil. The oil will help the seasoning adhere. Season all over with garlic salt and the ras el hanout spice blend.

4 Set up your grill for raised direct cooking and stabilize at 300°F. Cooking at this temperature will allow the game hens to retain moisture while roasting but will also promote browning and crisping of the skin.

5 Place the planks on the grill. Budget about 2½ hours for the birds to cook, and start checking the internal temperature at the 2-hour mark. Cook until the temperature reaches 165°F in the thickest part of the thigh and the juices run clear.

TIP The grill plank itself makes for a stunning presentation. Carve the game hens right on their planks at tableside. Consider making grilled veggies to go with them, and serve them alongside the game hens on the planks.

BEER-BATHED KIELBASA AND KRAUT

This super-simple dish is terrific for an outdoor party. Prep work is almost nonexistent. Even better, this dish can just simmer on the grill throughout the party with little or no maintenance needed, freeing you to mingle with your guests.

Serves 12 as an entrée or up to 20 as an appetizer

½ pound bacon, diced

2 medium sweet onions, finely diced

1 (28-ounce) jar sauerkraut

2 (12-ounce) cans American lager beer

4 pounds kielbasa sausage

1 Set up your grill for direct cooking and stabilize at 350°F.

2 In an 8-quart Dutch oven set on the grill, render the diced bacon over medium heat until crispy, taking care that it doesn't burn. Use a slotted spoon to remove the bacon from the pan; set aside. Add the diced sweet onions to the Dutch oven and slowly sauté in the bacon grease until translucent. Add half the sauerkraut, the bacon bits, and 1 can of the beer, stirring to incorporate.

Rendering the diced bacon over medium heat.

3 Cut the kielbasa into lengths appropriate for your party then cut in half lengthwise. For appetizer portions, 2- to 3-inch pieces are perfect. For sandwiches, 5-inch slices are just right.

4 Briefly grill the kielbasa—about 2 minutes per side—to add flavor and to make a dramatic presentation with grill marks. Then add the kielbasa pieces to the Dutch oven and cover. There should be enough liquid that the sausage pieces are evenly dispersed and bathing nicely in liquid. Add the rest of the sauerkraut and half a can of beer, making sure there's plenty of liquid for slowly braising the

Grill the kielbasa to add flavor and make a dramatic presentation with grill marks.

kielbasa. (Go ahead—drink the rest of the beer while you wait for the flavors to come together.)

This dish can be eaten almost immediately after being assembled, but the flavors will intensify as the kielbasa braises in the liquid with the kraut.

TIP I like to put a lid on the Dutch oven and allow the flavors to mingle for a good 45 minutes to an hour before guests arrive. When hungry guests begin to clamor around the grill to see what's cooking, I remove the lid so some of the moisture escapes and the aroma of cooked kielbasa and kraut wafts about. I've found that this dish can sit almost completely unattended over medium heat for quite some time, as long as you keep adding beer as needed so it doesn't burn. Let it simmer with the lid off to intensify the flavors and leave your guests wanting more.

A Fish Tale

I love grilled fish! Really, most seafood—but it wasn't always that way.

I grew up near the water, where fresh seafood was abundant, but I had little or no interest in eating it. I was 26 years old before I had a dinner where the main protein was from the sea. I was on a business trip, and my boss had made reservations at a classic waterfront seafood restaurant in Seattle. When I ordered a steak, she immediately vetoed my selection. "When you're back home in Montana, you can order all the beef you want, but here in Seattle you are getting seafood," she told me. She informed the waitress that I'd have the night's special—blackened shark—and told me I was going to like it. And like it I did. Despite my initial apprehension, after that I had a much more open mind toward seafood.

At my next job, my boss was known for having an international palate. When Montana got its first sushi restaurant, back around 1999, he seemed to be scheduling a lot more sit-down meetings—all of them at the new sushi place. I'd only recently opened my mind to seafood in general, so *raw* seafood was really a test of my courage. At the first meeting I attended, his wife came along to make sure we tried the miso soup. I tried so hard to be brave and adventurous, but at that time little things like seaweed could make me gag. When they saw my eyes begin to water, they took it upon themselves to become my sushi mentors.

Over the next few months, they set extensive goals for me as a student of sushi, while holding themselves to a high standard as facilitators. I was instructed on some of the essentials: "Keep that rice out of the soy sauce. Ask the chef how the *uni* looks today. Under no circumstances let us catch you pouring your own sake!" They were tough but fair, and they never forced me to play Follow the Culinary Leader when it came to ordering.

I feel lucky that I had good people teaching me how to enjoy sushi. And I've learned that if it comes from the ocean and it's prepared properly, chances are it will be wonderful.

STRIPED BASS ON A SALT BLOCK

Recently my dad brought me some Atlantic striped bass, freshly caught on Long Island Sound. I had never tried striped bass, but it seemed I was under the gun to create something delicious with it. I remembered seeing a photo of fish grilled on a slab of Himalayan salt, and I figured I'd give it a try. Salt in slab form can hold heat or cold for a long time, so it has some interesting applications. In this case, the salt slab creates a nice searing surface for the fish, while allowing it to pick up the smokiness from the grill. Another benefit is that the salt block keeps the fish from getting caught up in your grill grate and flaking apart on you.

Serves 2

2 (5-ounce) striped bass fillets or similar firm white saltwater fish

½ cup prepared Italian dressing

SUV Seasoning Rub (page 16), or your favorite spicy rub

SPECIAL EQUIPMENT
salt block

1 It is important to allow your salt block to slowly heat up to the target temperature over a period of about 45 minutes. Placing the salt block on the grill while it is stabilizing minimizes the chances of cracking. Set up your grill for direct cooking and preheat it to 200°F for 15 minutes. Then raise the heat about 75°F every 15 to 20 minutes until it reaches 400°F.

2 Soak the striped bass with the Italian dressing to add moisture, and season with the SUV Seasoning Rub.

3 Place the fish directly on the hot salt block and grill for about 8 minutes. Turn the fish over on the salt block midway through; a spatula works great for turning the fish and keeping it intact through the grilling process.

4 Remove the fish from the grill and let it rest for a few minutes loosely tented in foil before serving.

TIP While the fish rests, I put sliced, seasoned veggies (yellow squash, zucchini, and sweet onion) on the salt block and grill them to a nice caramel color. (Interestingly, the salt block doesn't really seem to impart much of a salty flavor.) The simple fresh fish and vegetables offer the taste of summer in a single bite. The fish is firm, mild, and flaky, with punctuated flavors from the grill. And it seems like you can taste every sunrise and sunset in the veggies, naturally seasoned by summer's sunshine, rain, heat, and cold. I store those flavors in my memory bank as a reminder of how special the short summer months are in the Mountain West.

CHINOOK SALMON TWO WAYS

I went fishing for salmon in Idaho and did something unusual: I caught some fish! I normally practice catch-and-release trout fishing, but on this trip we were after spring Chinook salmon in the Clearwater River. High in beneficial omega-3 fatty acids, the Chinook is one of the most sought-after salmon for both flavor and health benefits. A fishing buddy told me, "Save the sauces and marinades for other species. The spring Chinook is best prepared simply with salt, pepper, and perhaps some dill." I took his advice and made salmon two ways on the grill.

SEASONED SALMON

As advised, my first fillet was seasoned simply: salt, pepper, dill, and fresh lemon. Cooking on a cedar plank adds a flavor to the fish with little or no worry that it will stick to the grill or fall apart. It takes about the same time as it would to grill directly on the grate. I soak my plank in water for a couple of hours before grilling. This can add a little steam to your cook and helps prevent the plank from bursting into flames.

Chinook salmon from Idaho's Clearwater River.

2 (6-ounce) salmon fillets
salt and cracked black pepper, to taste

3 tablespoons fresh dill or 1 tablespoon dried dill

SPECIAL EQUIPMENT
well-soaked grilling plank, like cedar or alder

 1 Set up your grill for direct cooking and stabilize at 375°F.

2 Season the salmon with salt, pepper, and dill.

3 Place the fillet on the plank, skin-side down, and set the plank directly on the hot grill grate. Cook without turning for about 8 to 10 minutes, depending on how well done you prefer your fish. The plank will almost certainly char and possibly even burn a bit, which is normal. You may want to keep a spray bottle of water on hand to spritz the plank if it turns from a healthy char into a minor conflagration.

BLACKENED SALMON

For my second salmon fillet, I used a method that has gained tremendous popularity on my grill of late: blackening. A huge advantage of blackening on the grill is that you can get to a much higher temperature than on most kitchen ranges. It's a fast, effective way to cook fish, and it brings diverse flavors to the franchise. Blackening often leaves a crispy, charred crust on your food, providing texture as well as flavor.

Serves 2

2 (6-ounce) salmon fillets

2 tablespoons Blackening Seasoning (page 14), or your favorite blackened seasoning

2 tablespoons vegetable oil

1 Set up your kamado for direct cooking and stabilize at 400°F.

2 Lightly dredge the salmon in the seasoning mixture.

3 Preheat a cast-iron skillet on the grill. Add the oil to the hot skillet. I cannot emphasis enough how important it is to use extra caution with the oil on the hot cast iron. Oil combined with a searing-hot pan and an open flame can be disastrous, so please be careful!

4 Starting with the skin side down, blacken the salmon fillets in the hot skillet for about 4 minutes per side, flipping them midway through to blacken both sides. The salmon skin should be crispy and can be removed before serving if not desired. A huge advantage of blackening on the grill is that you can get a much higher temperature than most kitchen ranges. Also, the blackening process kicks out a tremendous amount of smoke that isn't always welcomed in a domestic kitchen.

REVERSE-SEARED STEAK

When you order a steak, it makes a statement. It says, "I'm a go-getter and I get what I deserve." And doesn't winning a set of steak knives imply that you've won the pinnacle of all prizes—or at least the pinnacle of all consolation prizes? But even better is having the skills to cook a steak that is simply sublime. I have found that the best way to achieve steak perfection is by using a roasting thermometer. The method I use is often referred to as a "reverse sear," and it's the key to achieving consistent results. Instead of searing the steak first, you roast it in the grill at a moderate temperature and then finish with a high-heat sear.

Serves 2

2 (12-ounce) tenderloin steaks, or any other tender cut such as New York strip or rib-eye

Steak Seasoning (page 15),
or your favorite store-bought brand

1 Remove your steak from the refrigerator and let it sit at room temperature for about 45 minutes. Trim off any silverskin that's easily accessible. You can also cut off and discard any excessive bits of fat.

2 Set up your grill for raised direct cooking and stabilize at 350°F.

3 Season your meat about 10 minutes before you begin cooking. Insert a digital meat-roasting thermometer horizontally into the steak, about halfway up its thickness. Slide it in as close to the center as possible.

4 Start by roasting the meat indirectly—that is, not right over the flames. If your grill doesn't easily let you position the meat next to the flame instead of over it, the raised grate will distance it from the heat, allowing it to roast without being directly charred until you're ready to sear it.

5 The thickness and internal temperature of your steak will determine how long to roast the meat. Pull your steak off the grill at about 10°F below your desired doneness (see Temperatures for Cooking Meat on page 17); the meat will continue to cook after it is removed from the heat. Remove the meat thermometer and let the meat rest on a plate, loosely covered with foil, for a good 10 minutes. This allows the juices to redistribute.

6 Resist all temptation to cut into the meat, and instead go back to your grill and raise the temperature to between 500°F and 600°F. This will take about 10 minutes. You're prepping the grill to sear the meat. Be sure to take safety precautions when cooking at this heat: use long tongs and wear protective gloves.

Sear the steak for about 1 minute per side. This will give it a beautiful crust, additional grilled flavor, and fabulous grill marks.

TIP By monitoring the internal temperature of the meat, you know that it will be cooked to your desired doneness. Roasting the meat slowly enhances its flavor while keeping it juicy. The reverse-sear method takes the guesswork out of grilling the perfect steak. Now if I can just figure out how to pick the perfect wine to go with it.

SUPER-SEARED STEAK WITH WHISKEY MUSHROOMS

The beauty of this dish is that it's easy all the way around. The ingredients are simple to find, and no special cooking equipment is required. We've made this steak while staying at vacation rentals and friends' houses, and for unexpected guests who show up hungry. I've come to love making it outside on the kamado grill in a cast-iron skillet. There's something so primal and caveman about cast iron over hardwood lump charcoal! If you don't have the whiskey that's called for, you can use brandy or Cognac.

Serves 2

2 (12-ounce) steaks, such as tenderloin or New York strip

salt and cracked black pepper

1 tablespoon cooking oil

1 pat butter

2 cups sliced mushrooms of your choice

2 ounces (¼ cup) Pendleton Whisky, or your favorite whiskey

1 cup heavy cream

1 Let your steaks rest at room temperature for about 45 minutes before you begin cooking.

2 Set up your grill for direct cooking and stabilize at 400°F.

3 Liberally season your steaks with salt and pepper. Start heating a cast-iron pan on the grill. Add the oil to lightly coat the bottom. You want a fine layer of oil but not enough that it pools in the pan, so adjust accordingly. Heat the oil until it glistens but isn't quite to the point of smoking.

4 Drop each steak into the pan with a heel-to-toe motion, flopping it away from you to safely introduce it to the heat. The steaks will adhere to the hot, oiled pan. Their flavor is developing, so leave them alone and set your timer for 4 minutes.

5 When the time is up, be ready to flip the steaks. I prefer to use tongs, but a fork or spatula should work just fine. Here's a little trick: when the steak is off the pan during the flip, give the pan a quick swirl to redistribute oil where the steak was. This will promote even browning of the second side after the flip. Cook on the second side for an additional 4 minutes, or if you like your meat more on the rare side, remove the steaks from the heat after 2 minutes and let them relax in the hot pan.

6 Place the cooked steaks on a plate under a tent of foil to rest while you cook the mushrooms.

7 Pour off any leftover oil and return the pan to the grill. Add the butter and use a wooden spoon to loosen up the brown bits in the bottom of the warm pan; these will add a bunch of flavor to the mushrooms. After a couple minutes, add the mushrooms. Cook for about 4 minutes, swirling and scraping the brown bits to share their flavor with the mushrooms. Sprinkle a pinch of salt evenly over the mushrooms and cook for another 4 minutes. The salt will bring the moisture out of the mushrooms and help intensify their flavor.

8 After about 8 minutes, take the pan off the heat and add the whiskey. Be careful—if the pan is close to the grill, the alcohol will ignite and flame off. Add the whiskey away from the heat and the alcohol will evaporate in a couple of minutes.

9 Add as much of the cream as needed to coat the mushrooms well, but we're not making soup, so don't drown them. Return the pan to the grill and cook, stirring occasionally, reducing the volume of liquid by about a third. The mushrooms and whiskey cream sauce should develop a rich brown, almost mahogany color and a silky, vibrant, savory taste that will harmonize beautifully with the steak.

10 Stir any juices from the rested steaks into the mushrooms just before serving, and transfer the steaks to individual plates. I like to spoon mushrooms over about a third of each steak and let the rest fall off its side and onto the plate. Finish with a few sprinkles of cracked black pepper over the mushrooms, if you can wait that long before digging in!

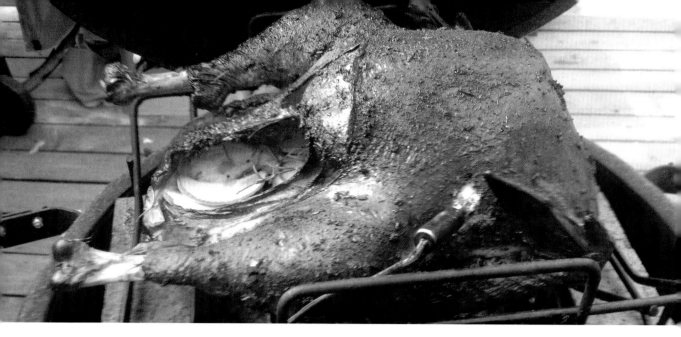

TURKEY ON THE GRILL, MONTANA-STYLE

Cooking a festive holiday turkey on the kamado grill is a great idea and for good reason. It comes down to flavor. You just cannot get as diverse a flavor profile by roasting a turkey in the oven as you can when you cook it on the grill. When it comes to seasoning, I prefer to use the Simon and Garfunkel method, utilizing parsley, sage, rosemary, and thyme that I pulverize and make into a paste with softened butter. I do my best to coat the bird liberally inside and out and carefully push seasoning under the skin of the bird as well.

I'm not a fan of putting stuffing inside of a turkey—it slows down the cooking process, and it can be tricky to achieve a high enough stuffing temperature for safety. No worries, though—you should have plenty of room for your favorite bread stuffing in your oven, which is probably getting pretty lonely by now.

Serves 6 to 8

½ cup loosely packed chopped fresh parsley

½ cup loosely packed chopped fresh sage

½ cup loosely packed fresh rosemary (stems removed)

½ cup loosely packed fresh thyme (stems removed)

2 tablespoons salt

2 tablespoons cracked black pepper

1 cup (2 sticks) butter, softened

10- to 12-pound turkey

4 cups chicken stock

2 cups diced celery

2 cups diced carrots

2 cups diced onions

4 bay leaves

1 Finely mince the parsley, sage, rosemary, and thyme with the salt and pepper, using a mortar and pestle or food processor. Mix with the softened butter.

2 Coat the bird liberally inside and out with the herb-butter mixture. Carefully push some under the skin as well.

Mince the herbs with a mortar and pestle.

3 Fill a Dutch oven about two-thirds full with the chicken stock, celery, carrots, onions, and bay leaves.

4 I set up my kamado grill a little differently when I'm cooking a turkey. I stabilize the grill at 350°F and use a roasting rack, which I rest on firebricks. I place the filled Dutch oven between the bricks and then set the roasting rack in place on the bricks. There are a few benefits to this setup:

Set-up for grilling a turkey.

- Raising the roasting rack lifts the bird high in the dome, which promotes more even cooking and will lead to beautifully browned and crispy skin.

- The Dutch oven with its liquid and spices provides a barrier between the hot coals and the bird, similar to what you get with indirect cooking.

- The liquid in the Dutch oven keeps a high humidity level in the Kamado while also catching any flavorful juices that leak out while the turkey cooks.

5 Place the turkey on the roasting rack breast-side up. You shouldn't have to baste the bird while it's cooking, but often I can't resist. Use a ladle, a turkey baster, or even a barbecue mop to get the job done—just make sure that the juices drip into the Dutch oven and not onto the hot coals.

Cook to an internal temperature of 165°F for the breast meat and 180°F for the dark meat, with juices running clear, about 15 minutes per pound. Loosely tent the cooked turkey with foil at room temperature for 30 to 45 minutes to allow its juices to reabsorb into the meat prior to slicing. If desired, strain the liquids collected in the Dutch oven and use them to make an amazing gravy with a rich smoky flavor. Although I have never had issues with the breast and dark meat getting done at different times there are two things you can do to prevent that if you wish.

- Remove the Dutch oven drip pan from beneath the turkey rack for the final 30 to 45 minutes of cooking to expose the darker meat to more heat

- Cover the turkey breasts and white meat area with ice-filled freezer bags for an hour at room temperature prior to cooking

TIP It is good practice to test the fit of your roasting rack, and drip pan, inserted probe thermometer, and any other accessories you plan to use prior to igniting your kamado. Please trust me that it will save you a lot of frustration later on in the cook.

TURKEY BALL DINNER

These reconstructed turkey balls are inspired by some of my favorite flavors from Thanksgiving dinner: turkey, stuffing, and a hidden cache of cranberry sauce. An absolutely delicious way to play with your food!

Serves 4

1 (14-ounce) can cranberry sauce

cooking spray

¼ cup finely minced onion

1 tablespoon minced garlic

6 tablespoons butter, divided

3 eggs, divided

¼ cup minced fresh parsley

1 pound ground turkey

1 teaspoon salt

1 teaspoon pepper

1 teaspoon onion powder

½ teaspoon Old Bay Seasoning

½ cup plus 1½ cups dry breadcrumbs

1 cup frozen Bacon Powder (page 16)

1 Place the cranberry sauce in a saucepan on the stovetop over low heat and allow it to slowly liquefy. Remove and let cool slightly, but not enough to re-solidify. Spray an ice cube tray with cooking spray and pour in the liquefied cranberry sauce; you'll need 4 standard-size cubes for filling the meatballs. Allow to harden in the freezer for 6 hours, or overnight.

2 In a small skillet, melt 2 tablespoons of the butter and sauté the onion and garlic on the stovetop over low heat until the onions turn translucent. Set aside to cool.

3 In a large mixing bowl, beat 1 egg with the onion-garlic mixture and the parsley. Mix in the ground turkey, salt, pepper, onion powder, Old Bay, and ½ cup of the breadcrumbs, using your hands to combine thoroughly (wear latex kitchen gloves). Cover and refrigerate for 1 hour to marry the flavors.

4 When you're ready to form and stuff the meatballs, remove the bacon powder from the freezer and break up any large clumps. Working quickly, add the bacon powder to the turkey mixture; use your hands to combine well.

5 Divide the mixture into 4 portions. Loosely form one of the portions into a sphere around one of the frozen cranberry cubes. Repeat the process with the remaining portions. Make the thickness of the meatball walls as even as possible—you don't want the cranberry sauce leaking out during the grilling process. Place the meatballs in the freezer for 40 minutes to firm.

Loosely form the turkey meat into a sphere around one of the frozen cranberry cubes.

6 Set up your kamado for raised direct cooking and stabilize at 375°F.

7 Melt the remaining 4 tablespoons butter in a small pan over medium-low heat on the stovetop. Remove from the heat and stir in 1½ cups breadcrumbs; set aside to cool. In a small bowl, lightly beat the remaining 2 eggs.

8 When you're ready to grill, remove the meatballs from the freezer. Dredge each meatball first in the beaten eggs and then in the buttered crumbs. A muffin pan with large openings works well as a cooking vessel for the meatballs but you can cook them on a baking sheet lined with foil as well.

9 Roast with raised direct heat for 35 to 45 minutes, or until the internal temperature if the turkey reaches 175°F. Carefully turn at least once to promote even cooking and browning.

BEHEMOTH CHIMICHURRI BEEF RIBS

Beef ribs were never my thing. But after reading a few posts in some online grilling forums, I figured I'd give these behemoth bones a try. I watched a famous chef make his version of a chimichurri sauce to slather over a large porterhouse steak, and I thought that would make a nice foundation for beef ribs. What's great about chimichurri is that it comes together quickly; with a little preparation and a rugged blender, you can whip up this sauce before your grill even gets stabilized.

Serves 6

1 large rack beef chuck plate ribs, about 4½ pounds

garlic salt
cracked black pepper

CHIMICHURRI MAYONNAISE

1 sweet onion, coarsely chopped	juice of 2 limes
10 garlic cloves	juice of 1 orange
2 shallots	juice of 1 lemon
1 jalapeño chile, seeded	1 tablespoon unseasoned rice wine vinegar
1 small bunch green onions, about 16	1 tablespoon Sriracha
1 cup chopped fresh parsley	2 cups mayonnaise

1 Remove the tough membrane beneath the beef ribs (see Prepping Ribs for the Grill on page 71). If you have a good relationship with your butcher, you can have this done when you purchase the meat.

2 Let the ribs sit at room temperature for about 45 minutes as you set up your grill for indirect cooking at 275°F. Hickory wood is a nice match for these hearty ribs; I mix a few chunks in with the hardwood lump charcoal at this stage. Be careful not to overdo it with the hickory wood; it has a very strong flavor that's best used sparingly.

3 Place a pan filled with 2 liters of warm water on top of your heat deflector under the grilling surface; a thick-walled, disposable aluminum pan works well. The water should be as hot as it gets from your tap. This will add moisture inside the kamado while also making cleanup a little easier.

4 Place all the chimichurri ingredients except the mayonnaise in a blender. Slowly pulse until a paste starts to form. Scrape down the sides as needed. If necessary, add water a tablespoon at a time so ingredients blend smoothly. Blend for 2 to 3 minutes, or until you have a consistent paste. Transfer the chimichurri from the blender into a medium bowl and whisk in the mayonnaise. Set aside.

5 Season both sides of the ribs with a good amount of the garlic salt and pepper. Using a large brush or spatula, paint about a third of the chimichurri mayonnaise onto the bottom side of the ribs. Then give an additional sprinkling of garlic salt and pepper to the bottom of the ribs with the chimichurri mayonnaise. Flip over and repeat on the top, using the rest of the chimichurri mayonnaise. Make sure that the chimichurri mayonnaise is spread evenly and there is no excessive clumping in any areas. Finish by seasoning the top side of the ribs with garlic salt and pepper.

6 Lay the ribs directly on the grill grate above the water pan. If your grill is well stabilized at about 275°F, there isn't much left to do other than to start getting very excited that these ribs will be done in close to 5 hours. From time to time, check your grill setup to make sure the temperature hasn't significantly spiked or dropped while you were enjoying the downtime.

Chimichurri-covered ribs ready for the grill.

TIP Ribs are done when the meat has receded from the thin end of the bone by ½ to 1 inch. You should notice portions of the ribs developing a gorgeous red smoke ring. There are various methods to test for doneness, such as poking the meat with a toothpick and seeing how much resistance you get. The less resistance, the more collagen and fat have broken down into tenderness.

Prepping Ribs for the Grill

Beef and pork ribs have a tough membrane underneath that is at the very least visually unappealing at the worst practically inedible. So whether you're grilling ribs for a few friends or for a high-stakes competition, you'll want to remove the membrane. Here's how you do it.

Use a round-tipped butter knife to get between the membrane and the bone by delicately inserting it near one of the middle rib bones. Work the butter knife an inch or so under the membrane and then switch to your finger to continue to loosen it from the bone. If it rips on the first try, switch to another rib. I like to work from the middle to one side, and then repeat. Grabbing on to the fickle membrane with a paper towel allows you to have much better leverage and grip.

Top Tips for Delicious Ribs

After many years of trial and error, I've developed some tips on how to produce consistently wonderful ribs. With all methodology, I encourage you to experiment, have fun, tweak, test, and try new things.

- Always remove the membrane from the bottom of the ribs—no exceptions. Be it beef or pork, the membrane is all but inedible, and I wouldn't be surprised if it was what was used to string together my catcher's mitt back in Little League.

- Slather your ribs with some kind of adherent. Typically I use mustard, but lately I've been combining that with mayonnaise, or using mayonnaise by itself. While this isn't completely necessary, I like the way seasoning rub adheres to the mustard or mayonnaise. Plain-Jane yellow hot dog mustard works best.

- Season the bottom side first—where you removed the membrane—and then season the top after you place the ribs on the kamado. I find this much less messy than trying to season both sides before I put my ribs on the grill.

- Use only fruitwood for smoking ribs. For pork ribs, I generally go with apple, cherry, or peach wood. I prefer to use less than 2 cups of woodchips, or no more than 2 or 3 small chunks—collectively no bigger than a truck-driver's fist. More may be better when it comes to bacon, but not with heavy smoke on your ribs. A small amount will still develop fantastic flavor and most likely leave your meat with an honorable pinkish-red smoke ring.

- Use a hot-water bath under your ribs. I use a pan that holds a little more than a 2-liter bottle of water, and I pour in the water as hot as it will come out of the tap.

- When you put your ribs on the grill (with the bottom side seasoned), position them over your water pan. After you have the rack aligned, squish the ribs together as best you can, like an accordion being squeezed. Bunching the ribs a bit will result in a taller, meatier presentation.

- Cook your ribs at 275°F for 5 hours or at 300°F for 4 to 4½ hours. If guests are getting antsy or you're getting hungry, wrapping the ribs in a few layers of heavy-duty foil with a sauce will dramatically break down the connective tissue toward the end of the cook.

- I don't sauce, foil, flip, or fuss too much anymore when I cook ribs. You learn at Kansas City Barbecue Society judging school that barbecued meat should recede from the bone by about 30 percent, and I often use that visual as an indication of doneness.

- Most important of all, have fun cooking ribs! The more you enjoy the cooking process, the more your guests will rave about how wonderful your food tastes.

COMPETITION-STYLE PORK RIBS

Here is a recipe I've used to make magnificent pork ribs. I advise bringing the entire roll of paper towels to the dinner table.

Serves 4

1 (4-pound) rack baby back pork ribs

½ cup Alpine Touch All-Purpose Seasoning

1 cup yellow mustard

½ cup Code 3 Spices Grunt Rub

½ cup Code 3 Spices 5-0 Rub

1 Remove the membrane from the bottom of the ribs (see Prepping Ribs for the Grill on page 71). Season the side where you removed the membrane with the Alpine Touch All-Purpose Seasoning.

2 Let the ribs sit at room temperature for about 45 minutes as you prepare your grill for indirect cooking. Use up to 2 cups of fruitwood chips or 2 or 3 small chunks, collectively no bigger than a truck driver's fist. Stabilize the grill at 275°F. Place a pan containing 2 quarts of warm water on top of your heat deflector under the grilling surface.

3 Slather the ribs with the mustard. Now season them all over with the Code 3 Spices Grunt Rub. I like the way the large granules coat the schmear. After that, use the Code 3 Spices 5-0 Rub. It's both sweet and zesty and works incredibly well with the other flavors.

4 Lay the ribs directly on the grate above the water pan with the bony side down and cook for 5 hours. When they are done to your liking, it's time to set the table. Allow to rest for 10 minutes before slicing. If you prefer your ribs to be fall-off-the-bone tender, double wrap them in foil for the last 45 minutes of cooking.

HICKORY-SMOKED BEEF TRI-TIP

Of all the methods I've tried for cooking beef tri-tip, this hickory wood-smoked recipe is what I go back to time and time again. It's not complicated, which really allows the beef to be the main event.

Serves 4 to 6

2½-pound tri-tip beef roast   SUV Seasoning Rub (page 16), to taste

1 Pat the roast dry with paper towels, season it with a generous amount of the rub, and place it in the refrigerator while you prepare the kamado grill.

2 Set up your kamado for raised direct cooking and stabilize at 325°F. I like to add 1 or 2 chunks of hickory wood—each about the size of a golf ball—close enough to the coals that they begin to smoke, but not immersed in the glowing heat so they flame and burn.

3 A digital probe thermometer for roasting is the key to nailing this recipe. Try to find the center of the meat horizontally and vertically, and insert the probe to run directly into this bull's-eye.

4 Set the tri-tip on the grill and slowly roast it, checking the thermometer readout about every 5 to 10 minutes. At first the temperature will climb quite slowly. But as it climbs to 90°F and above, you'll notice that it accelerates more rapidly. At about the 90°F mark, flip your meat to allow both sides to develop a gorgeous and flavorful crust.

Slowly roast to an internal temperature of 121°F for medium-rare meat. Generally this will take 35 to 40 minutes.

5 Remove the tri-tip from the kamado, set it on a platter, and cover it with foil to rest for up to 20 minutes or so. Leave the thermometer probe inside. The temperature will continue to rise and then settle somewhere between 132°F and 135°F, which is called "carryover." The faster you roast your meat, the greater the carryover.

6 Remove the thermometer and use a very sharp knife to slice the meat across the grain. The grain often runs in two or three directions; it's important that you cut *across* that grain.

TIP Using just a couple of small hickory chunks during the roasting process adds an extra dimension of flavor. Although it isn't absolutely necessary, it's a great way to layer your roast with nuanced flavor.

ZESTY NO-FRY BUTTERMILK CHICKEN

This marinated chicken stays extremely moist and has an unmistakable crunch when you bite into it. The chicken skin slowly cooks to a crisp shell that leaves you wanting another bite.

Serves 4

4 chicken drumsticks

4 chicken thighs

4 cups buttermilk

2 tablespoons garlic salt

3 tablespoons SUV Seasoning Rub (page 16)

2 cups panko breadcrumbs

¼ cup prepared Italian seasoning

¾ cup bruschetta-flavored olive oil, or olive oil flavored with 2 tablespoons Italian seasoning

1 Place the chicken pieces in a large zip-top bag. Carefully pour in the buttermilk, making sure all the pieces are covered. Add the garlic salt and SUV Seasoning Rub. Seal the bag and knead the chicken pieces in the buttermilk to distribute the seasonings as evenly as possible. Place the sealed bag in a bowl and refrigerate for 12 to 24 hours.

2 Mix the panko crumbs and Italian seasoning in a medium bowl. Transfer the chicken directly from the marinade bag into the crumb mixture one piece at a time, letting the excess marinade drip off before placing the chicken in the crumbs. Generously coat each piece with crumbs and set aside.

3 Set up your grill for raised direct cooking and stabilize at 275°F. This sounds low, but the chicken will be cooking for close to 2 hours. When the grill is well stabilized, gently arrange the chicken pieces on the grate, taking care to keep the breading as intact as possible.

4 Set your alarm for 25 minutes. When it goes off, check to see if the chicken is grilling evenly. Examine each piece to make sure it's not over an excessively hot spot. If a piece has significantly more color than the others, reposition it on the grill.

Brush the top and sides of all the pieces with the bruschetta-flavored olive oil. The oil will promote browning of the breadcrumbs and help the skin under the breading render to a deliciously crispy texture.

5 Close the dome and set your alarm for 35 more minutes. When the alarm sounds, it's time to flip the chicken pieces. Using tongs, turn each piece as gently as if you were placing a Fabergé egg in the case at Tiffany's. You've worked hard to adhere the crumb coating to the chicken—you don't want it falling off halfway through. Once all the chicken pieces have been turned, coat the tops with the flavored oil.

6 Now set your alarm for 45 minutes and go have a cold beverage. When the alarm goes off, your chicken should be about done. It's a choreographed waltz of preference at this point. By now the skin should be mostly rendered, the crumbs should be gorgeously golden, and the chicken should be cooked. Use a digital instant-read thermometer to check; 165°F is the minimum temperature any part of the chicken should be, but I'll bet you eclipse that by at least 5 to 10 degrees.

TIP I love chicken when it's still moist but has gotten firm, with most of the collagen and connective tissue melted away, so I'll probably leave it on an extra 15 minutes for a full 2-hour cook. You can decide just what degree of doneness you like—though once you've tasted this chicken, you may not be able to wait a full 2 hours.

RED PEPPER AND BACON-BATHED CHICKEN KEBABS

The red bell pepper, onion, and bacon powder marinade gives the chicken an amazing flavor you probably won't be expecting.

Serves 4

MARINADE
½ red bell pepper, cored

½ medium sweet onion

4 cloves garlic

CHICKEN
4 boneless skinless chicken thighs

1 tablespoon garlic salt

1 cup Bacon Powder (page 16)

½ cup dried Italian breadcrumbs

1 sweet onion, quartered

1 Place the red bell pepper, onion, garlic, and garlic salt into a food processor and blend until smooth. Fold the bacon powder and breadcrumbs into the mixture. Set aside.

2 Cut the chicken thighs into about 1-inch cubes (about 4 per thigh). Add to the marinade and marinate 4 to 24 hours in the refrigerator.

3 Start by skewering one of the onion quarters with the rounded side of the curve facing out, followed by a couple pieces of chicken thighs, and then a round side of onion facing inward. Think of the onions like parentheses that outline the chicken and hold the pieces from spreading on the skewer. Repeat, using 4 to 6 chicken pieces per skewer.

4 Set up your grill for raised direct cooking and stabilize at 375°F. Although you can cook directly on the grill grate, I like to balance the skewers on a couple of fire bricks, which elevates them from the grilling surface.

5 Grill the kebabs for about 45 minutes, until the internal temperature has reached 165°F and the marinade has developed a crisp texture. I prefer my chicken thighs a little more done and will often cook them to 180°F.

QUINOA AND GRILLED VEGGIES

Quinoa is hearty, filling, and fulfilling, with a comfort food quality to it. This grilled version makes an outstanding vegetarian main dish or side dish. It's perfect to put on the kamado toward the end of a slow-and-low cook, or even after your slow-and-low is done.

Serves 4

2 tablespoons butter

2 cups uncooked quinoa

4 cups low-sodium vegetable stock

2 cups finely diced grilled vegetables, from Grilled Veggie Quesadillas (page 31)

1 Prepare your grill for indirect cooking and stabilize at 350°F.

2 Once the grill is stabilized, set a 5-quart Dutch oven on the grilling surface. Add the butter and melt, and then add the quinoa. Sauté briefly, stirring, to incorporate the butter with the quinoa. Add the chicken stock and grilled vegetables. Give the mixture a stir and place the lid on your Dutch oven.

3 Cook the quinoa for 35 to 45 minutes. Grill times and temperatures can vary a bit, so keep an eye on it. Quinoa cooks similarly to rice; you want it to absorb the liquid, so don't stir or disturb it during the cooking process. When done, the quinoa should have a freshly sprouted look and a texture that's just past al dente.

TIP Enjoy this dish the way I like it best, in a bowl with a few roughly cut slices of Romano cheese on top. It also makes a great base for grilled marinated chicken breasts.

CHAPTER 3

VEGGIES AND SIDES

Vegetables don't get as much credit on the grill as they deserve. If you have access to a decent farmers' market or a backyard garden, you have opportunities for flavor that couldn't be achieved without using a kamado. Grilling veggies is often enough to enhance their flavors in an unexpected way. But sometimes—as with grilled salad—you transform something routine into something truly unique. The veggies and sides on the following pages are a true complement to any meal.

GRILLED SALAD WITH SHRIMP SKEWERS

Every once in a while, I get inspired to try something different or nontraditional on the grill. It's not that I go out of my way to try grilling things that aren't fond of fire; it's more of a why-not-throw-it-on-the-grill attitude that inspires me to try new things. Lately I've been working on the theory that grilled food just tastes better when it's cooked on a stick. My research is a work in progress, so the plan was to skewer up some shrimp before cooking them on the grill. I've found that the most versatile marinade and seasoning for grilling is Italian salad dressing. After the shrimp were skewered, they got a healthy slather of Italian dressing while my grill heated up.

Serves 2

1 crisp romaine lettuce heart

4 strips bacon

8 jumbo shrimp, shelled and deveined

½ cup prepared Italian salad dressing

¼ cup grape tomatoes, cut in half

¼ cup Cheddar cheese, crumbled

1 With thoughts of doing a nice wedge-style salad, cut the romaine in half lengthwise and remove the bitter stem from the bottom. Give the leaves a good rinse and set aside on a kitchen towel to drain and dry.

2 Set up your grill for raised direct cooking and stabilize at 375°F.

3 In a cast-iron skillet set on the grill, render the bacon until crispy. Remove and briefly grill the bacon directly on the grate to finish and firm up. Keep a careful eye on the bacon—if left unattended, it can go from zero to carbon very rapidly on a grill. Set the cooked bacon aside.

4 Thread 4 shrimp onto a skewer. Repeat with a second skewer. Place the skewered shrimp directly on the grate and grill for about 3 minutes per side. Generally, shrimp are done when they develop a deep pink color and lose their translucency.

5 Next slather the lettuce halves in Italian salad dressing; grill for about 2 minutes, until it begins to smell amazing and takes on a darkened, charred appearance in spots.

6 Transfer the grilled lettuce to individual serving plates. Crumble the bacon and sprinkle it over the wilted lettuce; add the grape tomatoes and cheese crumbles. Serve the shrimp skewers alongside the salad.

GRILLED CORN

In summer, our local food farm had fresh sweet corn. Enough said.

Serves 4

4 ears fresh corn, husks and silk intact

4 tablespoons butter, melted

1 teaspoon smoked paprika

1 teaspoon garlic powder

1 teaspoon minced fresh parsley

1 Set up your grill for direct cooking and stabilize at 400°F.

2 Make a grill butter by combining the melted butter with the paprika and garlic powder; keep warm.

3 Place the corn directly on the grill—husk, silk, and all. I try to put them near a hot spot but not directly over the hottest part of the grill. If you turn them a few times, allow the husks to develop an even char, and keep them from sizzling on direct heat, they should be done in 20 to 30 minutes. The husk and silk will peel off effortlessly.

4 Just before serving, stir the minced parsley into the grill butter. Brush onto each ear of corn.

HASSELBACK POTATOES

Seldom does a new interpretation of a basic old side dish excite me as much as this one. Called a Hasselback potato after the Swedish restaurant where it originated, this is a fancy version of the grilled baked potato. The concept is simple. Bake a potato on the grill, but first make some strategic cuts to expose its inner beauty.

Serves 2

2 russet potatoes, scrubbed   ¼ cup vegetable oil

1 Set up your grill for indirect cooking and stabilize at 400°F.

2 Lay a wooden spoon on a cutting board. Nestle a potato up against the spoon handle, which will serve as a template for how deep to make your cuts. Slice the potato from top to bottom as if cutting it into chips, but without going all the way through—the spoon handle will stop you. (If you're nervous that you'll cut through and ruin the potato, relax—it's a potato, not a lobster tail.) Repeat with the second potato.

Using a wooden spoon to cut your potato.

3 Rinse the cut potatoes and pat dry with a paper towel. Then brush them with the oil and place in a small pan suitable for roasting on the grill. Check in about 30 minutes to make sure they are cooking evenly and not being burned over a hot spot—your potatoes will be picking up wonderful grilled flavor and baking nicely.

TIP Sometimes I spread the potato slices apart and tuck a few pieces of pepper jack and Brie cheeses between the segments about halfway through the cooking process.

POTATO TOPPING

Here's a way to add flavor and crunch to your Hasselback potatoes.

¼ cup panko breadcrumbs

¼ cup grated Parmesan cheese

¼ cup melted butter or olive oil

1 tablespoon grated fresh horseradish

1 teaspoon garlic powder

1 Mix all the ingredients together in a small bowl. Sprinkle and pat onto the spuds after they've been roasting for about 1 hour and then cook for another 10 to 15 minutes. The oil in the topping will brown the crumbs and impart a nutty flavor. When the crumbs are golden brown and sizzling with melted cheese, remove the potatoes from the grill.

GRILLED FINGERLING HASSELBACK GERMAN POTATO SALAD SKEWERS

Using fingerling potatoes for this preparation does two things: it showcases just how sweet young potatoes are, and it allows for an appetizer-size portion for your guests to enjoy. With a few knife cuts, grilled and frilled fingerling Hasselback German potato skewers become as intriguing to look at as they are delicious to eat. The development of flavors between the vinegar, bacon, onions, herbs, and charcoal is pure magic. This makes an excellent accompaniment to a grilled breakfast as well.

Serves 4

½ sweet onion

⅔ cup cider vinegar

½ cup vegetable oil

1 tablespoon fresh cracked pepper

¼ cup chopped fresh parsley

4 strips bacon, cooked

16 to 20 fingerling potatoes

1 In a blender, purée the onion, vinegar, oil, pepper, and parsley together until a smooth mixture is formed. Break the cooked bacon into small pieces and add to the blender. Pulse until the bacon is finely chopped but still distinguishable. Pour the mixture into a container long enough to hold your skewers, such as an 8 x 12-inch Pyrex dish; set aside.

2 Slice the fingerling potatoes from top to bottom as if you were cutting them into chips, but don't cut completely through.

3 Thread the potatoes onto pairs of metal kebab skewers spaced about a finger's width apart, about 3 to 5 potatoes per set of skewers.

4 Steam the potato skewers for 8 to 10 minutes, so they are fully heated but not cooked through. I use a rice cooker for this, but you could also use a steam basket over water in a stockpot that has a tight-fitting lid.

5 Plunge the hot potato skewers into the marinade container. Let cool, then refrigerate for 4 to 6 hours or overnight to let the potatoes absorb the marinade flavors.

6 When you are ready to grill, set up your kamado for raised direct cooking and stabilize at 400°F.

7 Arrange the skewers on the grill and cook until the potatoes are crisp outside and tender inside, 30 to 40 minutes. Baste with the marinade 2 or 3 times. The potatoes should develop a rich, golden-brown color, and the slices will spread apart noticeably.

PROSCIUTTO-WRAPPED ASPARAGUS

Prosciutto-wrapped asparagus is one of those dishes that's just made for the grill. Working with the paper-thin prosciutto is a bit labor intensive, but this delicious appetizer or side dish is certainly worth the effort. If you are able to find young, thin asparagus, the contrast between the sweet asparagus and the salty prosciutto will be intensified.

Serves 4

1 pound slender fresh asparagus stalks   ½ pound thinly sliced prosciutto

1 Set up your kamado for raised direct grilling and stabilize at 375°F.

2 Cut off about the bottom third of the asparagus spears, leaving only the tender part of the stalks.

3 Cut the prosciutto slices into strips about 1 inch wide. Beginning at the cut end of the asparagus, wrap prosciutto around a stalk, overlapping the edges as you go until you reach the start of the asparagus tip. Repeat until you run out of asparagus or prosciutto.

4 Place the prosciutto-wrapped asparagus on the grilling surface perpendicular to the grate lines. (It should go without saying, but if you place your asparagus parallel to the grate bars, the chance of losing your creation to the fire gods is quite high.)

5 Depending on how hot your kamado runs, grill the asparagus for about 6 minutes, giving them a turn at roughly the 4-minute mark. The oils in the prosciutto will cause it to caramelize a bit and get crunchy, and some of the asparagus may blacken in exposed places. It will be up to you to determine what level of doneness, blackening, and caramelization you like.

TIP This recipe complements almost any main dish. For an extra treat, try cutting the grilled asparagus into half-inch pieces to top a salad. You may never go back to croutons.

GRILLED ARTICHOKES WITH CRAB CAKE STUFFING

Recently a few fresh artichokes lurked in my refrigerator, in desperate need of cooking. It was a warm day, and the thought of boiling them for a half hour made me wilt. I yearned to be able to cook them without creating more heat, so I reached for the seldom-used steamer function on my trusty rice cooker. The cooked artichokes made a perfect container on the grill for the crab stuffing from the Grilled Crab Cakes recipe on page 21.

Serves 4

4 artichokes

1 lemon, quartered

Grilled Crab Cakes mixture

½ cup sour cream, plain yogurt, or mayonnaise

1 To prepare the artichokes for cooking, use a sharp knife and kitchen shears to trim the stems, lop the tops, and snip off a few prickly leaf ends. To prevent darkening, rub the cut areas with the lemon pieces.

2 Snugly arrange the artichokes in a rice cooker. Pour about an inch of water in the bottom, toss in the lemon quarters, and set the rice cooker's steaming function for 30 minutes. A half hour later, the artichokes will be fork-tender, prepared perfectly without sweltering up the kitchen. Alternatively, steam or boil until tender.

3 Immediately drain off the hot cooking liquid and replace it with as much ice and cold water as the cooking pot will hold. The icy water essentially shocks the artichokes, locking in their rich green color and stopping the cooking. Let the artichokes soak in the cold water bath for at least 15 minutes.

4 Meanwhile, set up your grill for raised direct heat and stabilize at 400°F.

5 To prepare the filling, place the Grilled Crab Cakes mixture in a bowl. Gently fold in the sour cream, yogurt, or mayonnaise.

6 Drain the artichokes and transfer them to your work surface. Peel the leaves back to reveal the choke; use a fork to remove the inedible furry bits above the artichoke heart. Now stuff the cavities with the crab mixture.

7 Set the stuffed artichokes on the grilling surface. Cook for 20 to 25 minutes to let them pick up some smoky flavor and develop a crispy crust on top of the stuffing.

TIP Wherever an artichoke is cut or snipped, it instantly begins to oxidize and turn an unappetizing black color. This can be avoided by rubbing the cut areas immediately with lemon juice or a cut lemon. Cooks often throw a few cut lemon pieces in the cooking water for this reason, and for a little additional flavor. I suggest you do the same.

SMOKY SALSA

Salsa is so easily customizable that it's amazing anyone buys it at the store. One of the best parts about making your own is that you can easily change the flavor character, based on your mood or what you are serving. From July right up to the first frost, my salsa often is made from whatever the garden is producing. Tomatoes, onions, garlic, peppers, and chiles are obvious summertime choices. But other vegetables often get passed over when they could easily be included to add color, flavor, crunch, and nutrients. Don't overlook asparagus, carrots, radishes, kale, cucumbers, string beans, corn, herbs, and potatoes.

Serves 8 to 10

6 to 8 medium garden tomatoes, stemmed and cored*

2 medium jalapeño chiles, seeded and cut in half lengthwise

2 medium sweet onions

1 small bunch green onions, about 16

8 to 10 garlic cloves

olive oil

salt and pepper

2 teaspoons garlic powder

2 teaspoons onion powder

A firm tomato such as a Roma or an Amish paste tomato works well, but feel free to use whatever you have. Even a tomato that's not quite sweet enough to use in a salad will work fine for this salsa.

1 Prepare your grill for raised direct cooking and stabilize at 350°F.

2 Cut the tomatoes into quarters or thick slices, depending on their size. Do the same for the sweet onions. Thread the garlic cloves on a skewer and set aside.

3 When the grill has stabilized, brush all the veggies with olive oil and place them on the raised grate. Starting firmer-skinned veggies (such as the jalapeños and onions) skin-side down seems to work best. Sprinkle with salt and pepper.

4 You are aiming to soften the veggies and intensify some of the natural sugar flavors. The idea is to allow them to cook and caramelize without significant blackening or burning, so keep an eye on them. If a spot on the grill seems to be excessively hot, you may want to move things around a bit.

5 Doneness becomes a matter of preference at this point. Typically the onions will take longer to cook than the other veggies, but you may embrace the flavor of an al dente sweet onion and decide to leave it a little on the firm side. When the veggies are grilled to your liking, remove them from the kamado (this typically takes 5 to 10 minutes).

6 I purée the grilled tomato, garlic powder, and onion powder or pulverize them with a mortar and pestle as the base of my salsa. I hand-chop the rest of the veggies individually with a chef's knife on a wooden cutting board and add them to the puréed tomato as I go.

7 Serve with chips, carne asada, or even burgers.

TIP A blender, food mill, food processor, or immersion blender can make short work of the chopping if you prefer—but I think the salsa tastes best when I chop the ingredients by hand. It's part of the continuum of seed to fork that makes homemade salsa so tasty and satisfying.

GRILLED RICE AND RED BELL PEPPER PATTIES

Whenever possible, I try to balance my meals with a protein, a vegetable, and a starch. Contemplation led me to the freezer to fetch some ice for an adult beverage. When I opened the freezer door, a bag of frozen cooked rice left over from the other night stared me down, and then it hit me like a cattle prod. Can rice be cooked on the grill? Why not?

Serves 6

4 cups cooked jasmine rice, cooled

1 teaspoon onion powder

1 teaspoon garlic powder

1 teaspoon cracked black pepper

5 tablespoons diced red bell pepper

5 tablespoons finely diced tomato

1 egg

1 tablespoon Worcestershire sauce

1 tablespoon Sriracha

1 tablespoon soy sauce

5 tablespoons unseasoned rice wine vinegar

¾ cup panko breadcrumbs

cooking spray

vegetable oil

1 In a large bowl, mix the rice with the onion powder, garlic powder, black pepper, red bell pepper, and tomato.

2 Crack the egg into a medium bowl and whisk in the Worcestershire, Sriracha, soy sauce, and vinegar. When the mixture looks like a homogeneous salad dressing, pour it over the seasoned rice; stir to combine. Stir in the breadcrumbs to tighten up the rice mixture.

3 To make the patties, spray a 1-cup ramekin with cooking spray and pack it tightly with rice mixture. Upend the ramekin and slam it down onto a plate or baking sheet to dislodge the rice patty. Form 6 patties and place in the freezer for up to 1 hour to firm; this will help them hold their shape while cooking.

4 Set up your grill for direct cooking and stabilize at 375°F.

5 Brush the chilled patties with vegetable oil and place them on the grill. Cook for about 4 minutes per side. If you don't disturb them too much during the cook, the patties will hold their shape, the rice will brown nicely, and grill marks will appear. The rice will develop a wonderful crunch, with a rich sweetness and just a skoach of spicy heat.

CHAPTER 4

GETTING CREATIVE WITH THE KAMADO

The recipes in this section epitomize how I feel about creative cooking: they put a playful kamado spin on food, leaving a contagious smile on the face of anyone who gets a bite. From Game Day French Toast to get your grill going in the morning to a Bacon Tornado that leaves a wave of smoky goodness in its wake, these dishes will be as fun for you to serve as they will be for your guests to sample.

BAKED BRIE IN PUFF PASTRY WITH FRUIT

There's just something about serving baked Brie with fresh fruit that gets people excited. I once lived in a ski town where friends got together often for dinner parties; bringing this baked Brie always ensured an invite to the next event.

Serves 4 to 6

1 (17.3-ounce) package frozen puff pastry

1 (8-ounce) Brie wheel

1 egg

1 tablespoon water

1 apple, cored and thinly sliced

1 pear, cored and thinly sliced

2 cups strawberries, cored and halved

1 cup large blackberries

1 Remove the puff pastry from its packaging and allow to sit at room temperature for up to 30 minutes, or until malleable but still firm. Gently unfold the sheets.

2 Prepare your kamado for raised indirect cooking and stabilize at the temperature specified on the puff pastry package—typically 400°F.

3 Consider what you'll be baking the Brie on; you may want to prep the dish on that. I prefer to use a grill plank, which adds some flavor and makes for a dramatic presentation (a spritz of cooking spray on the plank prior to prep is never a bad idea). Or you can prep on parchment paper, transfer paper and cheese to the grill, and finally transfer the baked Brie to your serving platter with relative ease.

Position the Brie wheel on a sheet of puff pastry. With a sharp paring knife or pizza cutter, cut a puff pastry disk ¼ inch larger all around than the Brie wheel, for the bottom crust. Now cut a second disk the same size for the top crust. Cut a 1-inch-wide strip for the sides, long enough to go all the way around. By now the cut edges of the puff pastry should be a bit supple, and you will be able to adhere the top and bottom disks to the side strip simply by pinching the pieces together, creating a uniform pastry shell.

4 In a small bowl, beat together the egg and water to make an egg wash. Paint a thin coat of the wash on the top and sides of the puff pastry shell, taking care to avoid any pooling. The egg wash will promote browning and add visual appeal.

5 Bake the Brie on your kamado grill for as long as the puff pastry directions recommend, typically 20 to 25 minutes, or until the pastry is golden brown and airy.

6 Carefully remove the baked Brie from the grill. Serve it on the grill plank or transfer it to a serving platter, with fruit arranged alongside.

INSANE GRILLED OYSTERS

This is lots of fun to serve, because often people don't know what to expect when you grill oysters. Prep ahead of time so that you can enjoy a cold beverage while cooking. Grilled oysters demand attention—they cook quickly, radically change color, and give off an intoxicating smell that will make your neighbors jealous. This recipe can easily be doubled; after one bite, you'll wish you'd made more!

Serves 4

½ cup (1 stick) butter, divided

1 medium shallot, finely diced

4 cloves garlic, finely diced

¼ cup Col. Pabst All-Malt Amber Lager Worcestershire or your favorite Worcestershire sauce

¼ cup grated Parmesan cheese

¼ cup grated Romano cheese

¼ cup plus 2 tablespoons chopped fresh parsley

13 oysters on the half shell (an extra for the cook!)

1 In a sauté pan over medium-low heat on the stovetop, melt 2 tablespoons of the butter. Add the diced shallot and garlic and gently sauté until soft and translucent, 5 to 8 minutes. Add the remaining butter and let melt. Remove from the heat and pour into a medium bowl. Stir in the Worcestershire sauce. Cover and refrigerate, allowing the butter to solidify but not totally harden—about 25 to 30 minutes, depending on the refrigerator temperature. When the mixture has set, stir in the cheeses and parsley. Place in the refrigerator to firm.

2 Set up your grill for raised direct heat and stabilize at 550°F.

3 Scoop out about a tablespoon of the cold butter mixture and place on a cold oyster on the half shell. A melon baller or tiny ice cream scoop works well for this, giving you consistent topping amounts. Repeat for all the oysters.

4 Place the cold oysters, topped with the flavored butter, directly on your raised grill grate. Grill for 7 to 9 minutes, until the butter has melted and cooked the oyster in its shell. Check to make sure the cheese is fully melted and bubbly, evenly browned and crispy in spots.

Try to not cook the oysters so long that all the juices evaporate. Cooked perfectly, these oysters will be plump, juicy, and full of flavor.

GRILLED DESSERT PEACHES

The cool thing about grilling peaches is that no one really expects them, especially as a dessert. One of the benefits is that there's very little prep work involved, and what little prep is needed can be done as much as 24 hours ahead. Then just keep the peaches in the refrigerator until you're ready to grill.

I've actually found that peaches that are a little bit under-ripe work better for grilling than peaches at the peak of ripeness, dripping with juices.

Serves 4

4 peaches
ground cinnamon (optional)

½ cup Greek yogurt with honey flavor, for topping
granola and fresh mint leaves, for garnish

1 Set up your grill for direct heat and stabilize at 325°F.

2 To cut the peaches, hold stem-side up and slice from top to bottom about a half inch out from the stem. Your knife should cut all the way down, missing the pit completely. Repeat on the other side. Now slice off the narrow pieces of flesh left on each side of the pit. You'll have 2 large hemispheres and 2 narrow pieces per peach, ready for the grill.

3 Seasoning really isn't necessary, but if you wish, you can lightly dust cinnamon over the peach pieces.

4 Place on the grill cut-side down to allow for maximum surface exposure to the heat. Use your senses to monitor this dessert. The aroma will be amazing, but you'll be able to smell burning before it gets out of control if a piece is cooking over a hot spot. Avoid excessive blackening in the early stages of grilling.

If the peaches are firm, you'll notice that they get more supple as they cook. When this happens, it's a good time to flip. Try flipping once after 8 to 10 minutes, and decide if you need to flip again based on the char marks. The peaches are done when they get supple.

5 Serve simply, with a dollop of honey-flavored Greek yogurt and a sprinkling of granola. A bright mint leaf looks particularly gorgeous in contrast to the grill marks on the peach.

GAME-DAY GRILLED FRENCH TOAST

I love game-day cooking and have been known to plan a menu around whomever we are playing that day. The problem is that I just can't wait until kickoff to have something to eat. Recently, I decided to fill the pre-game void with breakfast on the grill. I had French toast on my mind. I'm not really much of an egg guy. If I have French toast, I prefer it with only a scant trace of egg dip, just enough to help it brown. It turns out that the dry heat from the grill works magically to impart flavor and texture without leaving any custardy egg residue.

Serves 2

3 eggs

¼ cup black coffee, cooled

¼ cup half and half

1 heaping tablespoon ground cinnamon

cooking oil for grill

4 slices country white bread

butter and maple syrup, for serving

1 Making sure the grilling surface is clean, set up your grill for direct cooking and stabilize at 375°F.

2 Crack the eggs into the bowl of a stand mixer. Using the mixer's whisk attachment, mix in the coffee, half and half, and cinnamon. Whisk until very frothy. Transfer to a shallow bowl and set aside.

3 Just before grilling, oil the grilling surface. Dip the bread slices in the egg mixture just long enough to soak up some of the mixture; immediately place on the grilling surface. You'll smell the cinnamon as soon as the bread hits the grill.

The kamado has an interesting effect on the bread—the bottom will sear over the intense heat, but the top will bake as if in an oven. Cook for about 2 minutes per side, keeping a close watch for any signs of burning. When done, the Fresh toast should be golden brown, crispy on the outside, and moist like fresh-baked bread on the inside.

4 To serve, top with a little butter and syrup—preferably real Vermont maple syrup.

TIP The combination of coffee and cinnamon is accentuated by the grilling. The smell of fall football is in the air! Grilled French toast and sausage is a huge win.

BACON TORNADO

This recipe was created for a contest at a local radio station. It's a whirlwind of bacony flavor, picking up any porky goodness in its path and leaving a devastatingly delicious mess of bacon flavor in its wake.

Serves 3

1 (6-ounce) pork tenderloin section

1 teaspoon smoked paprika

1 teaspoon garlic powder

1 teaspoon onion powder

1 teaspoon cracked black pepper

7 strips bacon, divided

¼ cup finely diced sweet onion

¼ cup grated Pepper Jack cheese

1 Pound the pork tenderloin to about a ¼-inch thickness. Season both sides with the smoked paprika, garlic powder, onion powder, and black pepper. Set aside.

2 Dice 3 slices of bacon. In a nonstick skillet on the stovetop, render the bacon over medium heat until it's deliciously crisp, taking care not to burn it. Lift the pieces out of the skillet and set aside on a paper towel–lined plate to cool. Drain off all but 2 tablespoons of the bacon fat. In the pan with the reserved bacon grease, sauté the sweet onion over low heat. Cook until translucent, then remove and let cool.

3 Set up your grill for indirect cooking and stabilize at 375°F. Add some applewood chips to the grill so the smoke can swirl around to create a kaleidoscope of flavor while the tornado is cooking.

4 In a medium bowl, mix the cooled sautéed onion, cooked bacon, and grated cheese.

5 Lay the remaining 4 bacon slices side by side on a clean work surface, like solders standing in formation. Place the flattened pork on top of the bacon, squared up with the bacon at one corner. Smear the bacon-cheese mixture onto the pork and roll tightly into a cigar shape. As you roll, bring the bacon along to wrap the tornado and cover the pork cigar, leaving nothing but bacon exposed.

6 Roast on the grill for 45 minutes to 1 hour, or until the bacon looks irresistible and the internal temperature of the pork is at least 155°F. Remove and let it rest for at least 10 minutes under a loose tent of foil, then slice into rounds and enjoy. Don't blame me if you want to make it again the day after tomorrow.

CHICKEN CORDON BLEU SOUS-VIDE

Ask 10 friends what their version of comfort food is, and be prepared to receive 10 answers. A common theme is that comfort food evokes passion, nostalgia, and memories of warm times spent with friends and family. For me, the meal that brings back the fondest of memories is quite simple—baked breaded, boneless chicken served with seasoned mashed potatoes and corn. Some sort of magic happens when the herbed breading mixes with the juicy chicken.

A variation on my most comforting of meals is stuffing the chicken with ham and Swiss cheese to make chicken cordon bleu. My thought was to re-create chicken cordon bleu with the cheese still in the middle but the salty ham on the outside—and to attempt to improve on a favorite dish with the help of the sous-vide cooking method.

For this new version, chicken thighs are substituted for chicken breasts, ham is replaced with prosciutto, and Gruyère takes the place of Swiss cheese. The assembled chicken bundles are vacuum-sealed and cooked for a prolonged period in a warm-water bath before being finished on the grill. It was fun to play around with a dish that I've always found so comforting. I have yet to decide if this is comfort food rediscovered, or if I just like to play with my food.

Serves 4

4 boneless, skinless chicken thighs

12 slices prosciutto

4 (1-ounce) cubes Gruyère cheese

SUV Seasoning Rub (page 16)

SPECIAL EQUIPMENT
food-sealing device

immersion sous-vide heater

1 Pound the chicken thighs to a uniform thickness of about ½ inch for even cooking.

2 Position two 14-inch-long pieces of plastic wrap on your work surface, overlapping them to form a cross. Arrange 2 prosciutto slices side by side in the center. Top with a chicken thigh, then place a piece of cheese in the middle of the chicken. Shake on some seasoning rub.

3 Lift two opposite corners of the plastic wrap and bring them together in the middle. Repeat with the other two corners to form a makeshift hobo knapsack filled with meat and cheese. Use the plastic wrap as a form to shape the meat into a tight ball; tie shut with string. Repeat with the remaining chicken thighs.

Form a makeshift hobo knapsack filled with meat and cheese.

4 Use a food-sealing device to vacuum-seal the chicken packets in a plastic pouch, or place them in a zip-top plastic bag and remove as much of the air as you can.

5 Preheat your sous-vide device to 165°F. Gently cook the chicken in the water bath for 1½ hours.

6 Set up your grill for raised direct cooking, adding up to 2 cups applewood chips. Stabilize at 375°F.

7 Remove the chicken balls from their plastic pouches and peel off the plastic wrap. Be careful—the wrapped chicken balls will come out hot! Pat the unwrapped chicken balls dry with paper towels in preparation for the grill. Then wrap another slice of prosciutto around each chicken ball.

8 Grill the prosciutto-wrapped chicken balls for about 35 minutes, rotating the pieces for even browning. While on the grill, a couple of things will happen: 1) the chicken balls will take on a sweet, rich, smoky flavor from the applewood smoke, and 2) the prosciutto will render a bit, absorbing smoke and forming a crunchy outer shell.

9 Transfer the chicken balls to a serving platter. When you cut into them, the cheese will ooze out, sharing its rich flavor with whatever it contacts.

TERIYAKI BEEF TENDERLOIN WITH GREEN ONION SKEWERS

Using green onions as skewers is a wonderful way to make an expensive cut of meat go a long way. Beef tenderloin can be grilled hot and fast, which won't overcook the beef but will leave a beautiful char on the green onions. This dish goes well with steamed jasmine rice and cold sake on a warm summer afternoon.

Serves 4

1 (12-ounce) beef tenderloin steak

2 or 3 bunches green onions (about 25 stalks)

1 cup Soy Vay Veri Veri Teriyaki, or your favorite teriyaki sauce

salt and pepper

sesame seeds and green onion slivers, for garnish

1 Use a sharp paring knive to remove any silverskin from the tenderloin. Cut the steak into slices no thicker than a pencil, and then cut each slice into strips 1½ to 2 inches wide. With a 12-ounce tenderloin steak, you should be able to get about 20 to 24 portions, depending on how careful you are with your cuts.

2 Set up your grill for direct cooking and stabilize at 400°F.

3 Slice off the roots at the bottom of the green onions. For a uniform look, I like to bunch up all the onions with the white bulbs together and then cut the green tops to the same length.

4 Poke 2 small holes through a tenderloin piece, about an inch apart, with a knife or chopstick. Thread a green onion "skewer" through the holes and slide the beef down toward the bulb end of the onion. Repeat with the rest of the meat and green onions. Sprinkle generously with salt and pepper.

5 Grill for 2 minutes per side. After flipping the skewers, immediately brush on a generous portion of teriyaki sauce so the flavors can begin developing. You can flip a second time to sauce the other side and then cook for another minute, but don't cook for longer than 5 minutes total. Some of the green onion will char, and some of it will roast. When grilled over direct charcoal heat, green onion releases a sweet and savory flavor almost reminiscent of umami.

6 Garnish with sesame seeds whimsically sprinkled over the beef along with wire-thin slivers of raw green onion.

TIP Wrapping the beef tenderloin tightly in plastic wrap and placing it in the freezer for 30 minutes before you slice it will make cutting even portions much more manageable—and allow you plenty of time to sharpen your knife.

CHAR SIU PORK

I have made this dish many times, and every time the same thing happens. I want to make it again immediately! Having always loved the balance of sweet, spicy, sour, and salty in Asian cooking, my taste buds thrive on the flavors of this dish. Char siu pork has been served to me at many restaurants.

This is a two-phase cooking process similar to the reverse sear (see Reversed-Sear Steak, page 60), in which the meat is roasted first and then hard-seared for additional flavor and texture.

Serves 4

1 (16-ounce) pork tenderloin

¼ cup soy sauce

¼ cup unseasoned rice wine vinegar

¼ cup hoisin sauce

¼ cup Sriracha, or to taste

¼ cup ketchup

¼ cup maple syrup

¼ cup cooking sherry

3 tablespoons sesame oil

3 tablespoons grated fresh ginger

2 tablespoons finely minced garlic

1 tablespoon cracked black pepper

1 tablespoon onion powder

1 tablespoon garlic powder

1 Prepare the pork tenderloin by cutting off and discarding any silverskin. Also peel away and discard any significant amounts of fat. Divide the meat into evenly portioned cylinders, making sure the sizes are as consistent as possible.

2 In a medium bowl, whisk together all the remaining ingredients until well combined. Place the pork pieces in a gallon zip-top bag and carefully pour in the marinade. Set the bag in a large bowl and refrigerate for 10 to 24 hours, rotating the meat inside the bag every 6 hours for even marinating.

3 Set up your grill for raised direct cooking and stabilize at 400°F.

4 Remove the tenderloin pieces from the bag, shaking off the excess marinade, and place on grill. Slowly roast the meat until it reaches an internal temperature of 138°F, about 20 minutes. Every 4 to 6 minutes, brush the meat with the leftover marinade. This forms a nice crust, and the aroma will make your neighbors want to return the leaf blower they borrowed last fall.

5 When you hit the target temperature, remove the meat from the grill and loosely tent with foil.

6 Slowly roasting the meat over raised direct heat often leaves a wonderful char and gorgeous grill marks. If these are to your liking, feel free to stop here. But if you prefer an extra-hard sear and charred crust, remove the meat then open the kamado vents and let the temperature climb to about 575°F, which I find ideal for a hard sear. Return the meat to the grill and sear over this high heat for about 45 seconds per side. Use all your senses to determine just how long to sear. Remember—there are sugars in the marinade, which will burn if left unattended.

TIP I like to thinly slice this grilled pork and fan it out on a plate or serving platter for all to enjoy. Make sure you sample a few slices while you're cutting, because they won't last long!

Kamado Grilled Pizza Setup

Pizza is a food group for me. It evokes more emotion than any other food that I grill on a regular basis. I've been grilling pizza for about three decades now, but pizza on the kamado has been a challenge. After three years of experimenting, however, I've found a technique that works well.

This grilling setup puts a substantial thermal mass between your pizza and the lava-hot hardwood lump charcoal. That makes the coals heat more evenly, and raising the pizza high in the kamado's dome promotes even cooking on the top and bottom.

- Start by taking a few minutes to completely clean out your kamado. Take out the fire ring, firebox, and anything else that's inside and clean out all the ashes. I prefer to use a shop vac for this, but an ash tool and dustpan work, too. Starting with a clean, ash-free grill is essential when you're cooking at high temperatures for any length of time.

- Put everything back together, making sure that the air intake opening on the firebox is aligned with the draft door, or whatever the ideal setup is for your cooker's unobstructed airflow. Fill the kamado to the top of the firebox with your favorite hardwood lump charcoal. I often dump the charcoal into the grill right from the bag, but placing larger pieces by hand in the bottom will provide a solid base for your heat while assuring maximum airflow.

- Light the kamado and allow it to come to a stabilized temperature of 450°F to 475°F.

- Once the heat has stabilized, it's time to add some thermal mass. Start by placing your heat deflector in the kamado with the legs facing up. It's imperative to have a heat shield that still allows for maximum airflow. Place your grate on top of the heat shield, and then set 3 firebricks close together on top of the grate. On top of the firebricks, I position the ceramic riser feet that came with my kamado—but empty tuna cans, a few stacks of quarters, or even a few balls of foil will work as spacers, too.

Place your heat deflector in the kamado with the legs facing up.

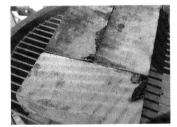
Set 3 firebricks close together on top of the grate.

Use ceramic riser feet to elevate your pizza stone.

- Place your pizza stone on top of the spacers. I really recommend investing in a rugged pizza stone. I've broken more than a dozen standard pizza stones over the years, while the one I bought from my grill manufacturer is still going strong after a hundred-plus pies.

- With your heat shield, grate, firebricks, spacers, and pizza stone in place, it's time to let them come to temperature for grilling your pizza. I recommend a minimum of a half hour for this (45 minutes would be better, but I feel that any longer than that is a waste of charcoal). Everyone has a different temperature that they consider ideal. Determining the right heat level has to do with how hydrated your pizza dough is and how much sugar it contains. A dough with higher hydration can handle hotter temperatures, while dough with more than minimal sugar has a good chance of burning before the pizza is done. My sweet spot is between 500°F and 525°F. Some people prefer to go much higher, but safety considerations for you and your guests provide enough of an incentive to keep your temps under 600°F. The kamado grill's gasket will thank you as well.

- I recommend that you roll out your dough on parchment paper. The parchment paper will make your pizza slide onto the pizza stone easily, whereas flour or cornmeal is susceptible to getting stuck if there's any moisture. Parchment paper can easily be removed a few minutes after you start grilling the pizza, or you can wait until just before the pizza is done. Pizzas typically cook for 8 to 12 minutes, depending on what level of doneness you prefer.

BACON PISTACHIO PIZZA

The amounts of the ingredients used in this pizza are at the discretion of the chef—adjust accordingly. Prep is relatively simple. The feta cheese is cut to the size of sugar cubes, and the pistachios are worked over with a chef's knife.

Makes 1 (14-inch) pizza

1 ball pizza dough for approximately a 14-inch pie

¼ cup olive oil

1 cup grated mozzarella cheese

4 ounces fresh mozzarella cheese, cut into about 8 pieces

16 kalamata olives, pitted

12 feta cheese cubes

½ cup roughly chopped pistachios

3 tablespoons Bacon Powder (page 16)

1 Set up your grill according to the instructions on page 119.

2 Roll out the pizza dough on parchment paper to about a 14-inch circle.

3 Spread olive oil over the entire surface and sprinkle with the grated mozzarella. Distribute the remaining toppings evenly over the pizza, using a deft hand to make sure that you'll be able to enjoy as many flavors as possible with each bite.

4 Transfer the pizza to the kamado and grill for 8 to 12 minutes.

SHRIMP SCAMPI PIZZA

Makes 1 (14-inch) pizza

5 shrimp (extra jumbo, colossal, or U-12), shelled and deveined

2 strips bacon, roughly chopped

1 ball pizza dough for approximately a 14-inch pie

¼ cup extra-virgin olive oil

1 tablespoon garlic powder, or to taste

2 tablespoons minced garlic

¼ cup grated Parmigiano-Reggiano cheese

½ cup grated mozzarella cheese

2 tablespoons finely diced red bell pepper

2 tablespoons minced fresh parsley

1 Set up your grill according to the instructions on page 119.

2 Cut the shrimp in half lengthwise along the line where the vein was removed; this will allow them to cook a little faster. Set aside.

3 Raw bacon doesn't cook properly on a pizza, so I par-cook it first. In a medium skillet set over medium-low heat on the stovetop, sauté the chopped bacon for about 6 minutes so that it's about two-thirds cooked and most of the fat has been rendered off. Remove the bacon from the pan and set aside.

4 Roll out the pizza dough on parchment paper to a rough 14-inch circle.

5 Pour the olive oil onto the pizza dough and spread evenly across the top. Lightly sprinkle garlic powder and then minced garlic evenly over the dough. Distribute the Parmigiano-Reggiano cheese across the pizza and follow with a layer of mozzarella.

6 Evenly distribute the shrimp halves on top of the cheese. Sprinkle on bacon bits and red bell pepper. Finishing the par-cooked bacon on the pizza will release some of the bacon's fats and flavors, making for an unmistakably delicious pie.

7 Transfer the pizza to the grill and cook for 8 to 12 minutes, until the shrimp are done, the cheeses are well melted, and the crust is a crispy golden brown. Sprinkle on minced parsley after slicing at tableside.

TIP Ingredient amounts depend on personal preferences. If I'm serving this pizza to someone who doesn't like garlic as much as I do, I'll lightly sauté the garlic in olive oil first and use a smaller amount on the pizza.

GLUTEN-FREE DESSERT PIZZA

Recently a friend asked me if I knew of any good gluten-free desserts that could be grilled. I didn't—so I decided to make a gluten-free grilled dessert pizza highlighting some of my favorite sweet summer flavors. I've always wanted to make a pizza-size chocolate chip cookie on the grill, and I thought that would make a fantastic crust.

Where I live in western Montana, the wild huckleberries are as sweet as can be. They have a much stronger smell and taste than blueberries and are much juicier. Peaches often go on the grill under-ripe—crunchy and rather bland. It's satisfying to watch them caramelize and become sweeter and softer over the charcoal heat. In this pizza's topping, the sweetness of the huckleberries and grilled peaches is balanced by the slightly sour and creamy richness of mascarpone cheese.

Serves 8

1 gluten-free chocolate chip cookie mix (such as Bob's Red Mill Gluten Free Chocolate Chip Cookie Mix)

3 peaches

2 cups (16 ounces) mascarpone cheese

1 cup wild huckleberries (fresh or canned) or a favorite seasonal berry

¼ cup honey

1 Set up your grill for indirect cooking and stabilize at the temperature suggested on the cookie mix package. This giant cookie will be baked on a 16-inch pizza stone, so be sure to let the stone warm up for at least 50 minutes while the grill stabilizes.

2 Prepare the cookie dough according to the package directions. I followed the directions on a bag of Bob's Red Mill Gluten Free Chocolate Chip Cookie Mix and combined the ingredients using a stand mixer. The directions called for mixing for 2 minutes, but at that point my dough resembled soft, wet sand. I let the mixer slowly do its thing, and at about the 5-minute mark it came together in a cohesive ball.

3 Press the cookie dough between sheets of parchment paper and roll it into about a 10-inch circle. Remove the top sheet of parchment paper and transfer the dough circle onto the preheated pizza stone.

4 Grill for the time specified on the cookie package. (However, it's good to check before the suggested time is up; the Bob's Red Mill mix said to bake for 12 to 14 minutes, but when I checked at 10 minutes the cookie had spread to a 14-inch circle. This was quite a bit more than I'd planned for, but fortunately my pizza stone had room to spare.) When the cookie is done, remove it from the grill to cool.

Grill the cookie for the time specified on the package.

5 Slice the peaches into thick wedges and grill at 350°F, cut-side facing the grill grate, for 12 minutes. Then flip and grill for another 12 minutes. Remove and let cool.

6 Using a stand mixer, blend the mascarpone, berries, and honey into a spread. The cheese will be stained purple from the berries and will smell wonderful.

7 Spread the mascarpone-huckleberry cheese over the big cookie crust. Slice the peaches thinly and spread over the top so there will be a taste of peaches in every bite. Use a sharp chef's knife to cut the dessert pizza into slices.

TIP Building a multilevel taste experience is important so that you first get a blast of sweetness from the peaches but then pick up some savory grilled flavor. Texturally the mascarpone-huckleberry spread plays perfectly off the softened peaches, followed by the crunch of the cookie crust. Your mouth goes through the same happy range of emotions as a slugger who knocks one out of the park, touching all the bases before reaching home. The next time you're looking for a grand slam of a dessert, give the Gluten-Free Dessert Pizza a shot.

CONVERSION CHARTS

VOLUME CONVERSIONS

U.S.	U.S. Equivalent	Metric
1 tablespoon (3 teaspoons)	½ fluid ounce	15 milliliters
¼ cup	2 fluid ounces	60 milliliters
⅓ cup	3 fluid ounces	90 milliliters
½ cup	4 fluid ounces	120 milliliters
⅔ cup	5 fluid ounces	150 milliliters
¾ cup	6 fluid ounces	180 milliliters
1 cup	8 fluid ounces	240 milliliters
2 cups	16 fluid ounces	480 milliliters

WEIGHT CONVERSIONS

U.S.	Metric
½ ounce	15 grams
1 ounce	30 grams
2 ounces	60 grams
¼ pound	115 grams
⅓ pound	150 grams
½ pound	225 grams
¾ pound	350 grams
1 pound	450 grams

TEMPERATURE CONVERSIONS

Fahrenheit (°F)	Celsius (°C)
200°F	95°C
225°F	110°C
250°F	120°C
275°F	135°C
300°F	150°C
325°F	165°C
350°F	175°C
375°F	190°C
400°F	200°C
425°F	220°C
450°F	230°C

INDEX

Accessories, 9–11

Airflow, 4

Appetizers, 19–45

Ashes, 12; removal, 8

Atomic Buffalo Turd, 24

Bacon, 23–25, 26–27, 111–12. *See also* Bacon powder

Bacon Pistachio Pizza, 121–22

Bacon Powder, 16, 79–80, 121–22

Bacon Tornado, 111–12

Bacon-Wrapped Jalapeños Four Ways, 23–25

Baked Brie in Puff Pastry with Fruit, 102–103

Bands, on kamado, 8

Beef, 60–61, 62–63, 74–75, 115–16; corned, 67–68; ribs, 38–39, 69–71, 72

Beer-Bathed Kielbasa and Kraut, 53–55

Behemoth Chimichurri Beef Ribs, 69–71

Blackened Salmon, 59

Blackening Seasoning, 14

Breakfasts, 108–109

"Burping" the grill, 12

Char Siu Pork, 117–18

Charcoal, 4–5

Charcoal ignition sticks, 5

Cheese, 44–45, 102–103

Chicago-Style Pigs in a Blanket, 29–30

Chicken, 40–41, 77–78, 79–80, 113–14

Chicken Cordon Bleu Sous-Vide, 113–14

Chimney starters, 5

Chinook Salmon Two Ways, 58–59

Citrusy Lemongrass Pork Satay, 42–43

Cocktail franks, 28, 29–30

Coffee Seasoning Rub, 15

Competition-Style Pork Ribs, 73

Conversion charts, 128–29

Cooking methods, 5–7; pizza, 7, 119–20; turkey, 65

Corn dogs, 28

Crab, 21, 94–95

Crab Cake Stuffing, 94–95

Creative dishes, 101–27

Cutting method, with wooden spoon, 88

Desserts, 106–107, 125–27

Direct cooking, 6

Duck Confit Egg Rolls, 37

Dutch oven, 11

Egg rolls, 35–37

Entrees, 47–81

Equipment, 3, 9–11

Eyewear, protective, 12

Fire safety, 11–12, 36, 39

Fish, 56–57, 58–59

Flanken-Cut Beef Short Ribs, 38–39

Flashbacks, 12

Fuel, 4–5

Game-Day Grilled French Toast, 108–109

Game hens, 51–52

Gaskets, on kamado, 8

Gloves, 10

Gluten-Free Dessert Pizza, 125–27

Green Onion Skewers, 115–16

Grill Plank Game Hens, 51–52

Grill planks, 11

Grilled Artichokes with Crab Cake Stuffing, 94–95

Grilled Caprese Salad Bites, 44–45

Grilled Corn, 87

Grilled Crab Cakes, 21

Grilled Dessert Peaches, 106–107

Grilled Fingerling Hasselback German Potato Salad Skewers, 90–91

Grilled Rice and Red Bell Pepper Patties, 98–99

Grilled Salad with Shrimp Skewers, 85–86

Grilled Veggie Quesadillas, 31–33

GrillGrates, 10

Hardwood lump coal, 4–5; reusing, 12

Hasselback Potatoes, 88–89

Heat deflectors/shields, 9

Hickory-Smoked Beef Tri-Tip, 74–75

Hinges, on kamado, 8

Indirect cooking, 7

Insane Grilled Oysters, 104–105

Jalapeño Taco Boats, 26–27

Jalapeños, 23–25, 26–27

Kamado grill, 3–12; cooking methods, 5–7, 65, 119–20; equipment, 3, 9–11; fuel, 4–5; illustrated, 3; maintenance, 8; safety issues, 11–12, 36, 39

Kebabs, 79–80

Lighting coal, 4–5

M-80 Jalapeños, 25

Main dishes, 47–81

Maintenance, of kamado, 8

Measurement conversions, 128

Mini Muffin-Tin Corn Dogs, 28

Moscow Mule Brined Pork Chops, 49–50

Oysters, 104–105

Pigs in a Blanket, 29–30

Pizza stones, 10

Pizzas, 121–22, 123–24, 125–27; grilling setup, 7, 119–20

Planks, wood, for grilling, 11

Pork, 42–43, 49–50, 111–12, 117–18; ribs, 73. *See also* Bacon; Bacon powder

Pork Marinade, 42–43

Pork Rub Seasoning, 13

Potato Topping, 89

Poultry. *See* Chicken; Game hens; Turkey

Prosciutto-Wrapped Asparagus, 92–93

Quesadillas, 31–33

Quinoa and Grilled Veggies, 81

Raised direct cooking, 6

Raised indirect cooking, 7

Ras el Hanout Spice Blend, 14

Recipes, 19–127; breakfasts, 108–109; creative dishes, 101–27; desserts, 106–107, 125–27; main dishes, 47–81; snacks/appetizers, 19–45; vegetable/side dishes, 83–99

Red Pepper and Bacon-Bathed Chicken Kebabs, 79–80

Reverse-Seared Steak, 60–61

Ribs: beef, 38–39, 69–72; pork, 73; preparation, 71–72

Safety issues, 11–12, 36, 39

St. Patrick's Day Egg Rolls, 35–36

Salmon, 58–59

Salsa, 96–97

Salt blocks, 10–11

Satays, 42–43

Sausage, 53–55. *See also* Cocktail franks

Seasoned Salmon, 58–59

Seasoning recipes, 13–16

Shrimp, 25, 85–86, 123–24

Shrimp Scampi Pizza, 123–24

Shrimp-Stuffed Jalapeños, 25

Sicilian Pizza-Stuffed Jalapeños, 24

Side dishes, 83–99

Skewers, 85–86, 90–91, 115–16

Smoky Salsa, 96–97

Snacks, 19–45

Sparks, while cooking, 12

Spatulas, 9

Stabilization, of grill, 5

Steak Seasoning, 15

Striped Bass on a Salt Block, 56–57

Super-Seared Steak with Whiskey Mushrooms, 62–63

SUV Seasoning Rub, 16

Temperature chart, meat cooking, 17

Temperature conversions, 129

Teriyaki Beef Tenderloin with Green Onion Skewers, 115–16

Thermometers, 10

Tongs, 9

Tools, 9–11

Turkey, 64–66, 67–68; grilling setup, 65

Turkey Ball Dinner, 67–68

Turkey on the Grill, Montana-Style, 64–66

Vegetable dishes, 83–99

Vegetarian dishes, 31–33, 44–45, 81, 87, 88–89, 98–99, 102–103; breakfast, 108–109; dessert, 106–107; salsa, 96–97

Vent screens, on kamado, 11–12

Volume conversions, 128

Weight conversions, 128

Wood planks, for grilling, 11

Wooden spoon cutting method, 88

Zesty No-Fry Buffalo Chicken Croquettes, 40–41

Zesty No-Fry Buttermilk Chicken, 77–78

ACKNOWLEDGMENTS

I have been fortunate to network with some amazing people who have supported me in many ways while writing this book. Chris Grove of Nibble Me This and author of *The Kamado Smoker and Grill Cookbook*, Robyn Lindars of GrillGirl.com, Dennis Linkletter of Komodo-Kamado grills, Sebastian Bussert of FOGO hardwood lump charcoal, and Michael Radosevich of Code 3 Spices have all made themselves available as tremendously valuable resources for this project.

I appreciate the patience of a few local butcher shops that have accommodated my constant requests for random cuts of meat used in my culinary experiments.

Special acknowledgment goes to my writing coach, sous chef, head cheerleader, taste tester, and best friend Chery Sabol. Her encouragement, patience, love, and support fuel my passions and make me want to excel at everything I do.

ABOUT THE AUTHOR

Grill master **Paul Sidoriak** created the website GrillingMontana.com to showcase his culinary successes and failures on the grill. Knowing that cooking is a creative or artistic outlet for some people, Paul uses his grill as a blank canvas. His grilling style is lighthearted, whimsical, and seasonally based, taking advantage of what is in season whenever possible. Some of his favorite creations take much less planning, prompted by his playful curiosity and the simple challenge of "What if ...?"

Paul has been known to fire up his kamado cooker almost 300 times each year, regardless of whether Mother Nature decides to cooperate at his home in western Montana. Follow what Paul has cooking on Instagram @GrillingMontana, Twitter @ GrillingMontana, or on Facebook at www.facebook.com/GrillingMontana.